北方少林
七星螳螂派
趙志民授徒李錦榮
李錦榮國術體育會

THE SECRET OF SEVEN-STAR MANTIS STYLE

Lee Kam Wing Martial Art Sports Association, 1985

©*All rights reserved. No part of this book may be reproduced in any form or by any means, without permission in writing from the publisher*

First Edition .... November 1985

Second Edition .... April 1993

Third Edition .... December 1996

Forth Edition .... March 1999

Distributor : Lee Kam Wing Martial Art Sports Association.
1, Un Chau Street., Block"B" Sham Shui Po, Kowloon, Hong Kong.

Printed by : Tung Mei Printing Products Ltd.
Unit 06, 9/F., Golden Ind. Bldg.,
16-26 Kwai Tak Street, Kwai Chung,
N.T. Hong Kong.

ISBN 962-8280-01-X

Printed in Hong Kong

THE SECRET OF SEVEN-STAR MANTIS STYLE

PUBLISHED BY
Lee Kam Wing Martial Art Sports Association

EXPLAINED WITH DIAGRAMS BY
Master Lee Kam Wing

Hong Kong Chinese Martial Art Association Permanent Member.
Hong Kong Chin Woo Athletic Association Director &
Seven-Star Mantis Kung Fu Instructor.
China Guangzhou Chin Woo Athletic Association Consultant.
As Director Of The British Tai Gi Quan And Shaolin Kung Fu Association.
Hong Kong Coaching Committee Coach Accreditation.
Singapore San Cheen Do Institute Over Sea Consultant.
Guardianship Of Germany Seven-Star Mantis Group.
Graduate From Chinese Acupuncture Medicine Institute.
Graduate From College Of Traditional Chinese Medicine.
Shaolin Temple Seven-Star Mantis Kung Fu Lee Kam Wing Martial Art Sports Association President.
Chinese Herbalist & Kung Fu Instructor.

TRANSLATED BY
Lee Kam Hoi
B. Sc.,

LEE KAM WING MARTIAL ART SPORTS ASSOCIATION
Headquarter: 1, Un Chau Street, 1/F., Block 'B', Shamshuipo, Kowloon, Hong Kong.
TEL.: (852) 2777 2161

Preface

The Northern Shaolin Seven-Star Mantis Style Master Lee Kam Wing who is the close-door disciple of Grandmaster Chiu Chi Man of the Ching Wu Athletic Association which was found earliest in Hong Kong.

Master Lee collected his achievement both from teaching and studying in the past twenty years. After four years in arranging materials for writing a book of his own decription he decided to publish 'THE SECRET OF SEVEN–STAR MANTIS STYLE' which is promoted to enhance and glorify the conventional spirit of Chinese Matial Art (Chinese Kung Fu) as well as a reference for people in the world who is interested in taking a self-study of the Seven-Star Mantis Style in Chinese Martial Art.

It is grateful to acknowledge that The publication of 'THE SECRET OF SEVEN–STAR MANTIS STYLE' has already gained permit from Grandmaster Chiu Chi Man who is now living in Hong Kong.

Details of The Secret of the Seven-Star Mantis Style including complete set of practising procedure such as The Principle of Stances; Fist-fighting technique; Palm-fighting technique; Leg-kicking method; The introduction of the real contact in Free-fighting competition and self-defence; The Seven-Star Mantis Style practising series from junior level to advance level which is demonstrated personally by Master Lee with detailed description, giving students a systematic method of practising The Seven-Star Mantis Style.

Besides, This book also introduce The Iron-Sand Palm practising; The use of Chinese medical prescription for physical strength traning; The Method of Wooden Dummy practising; The respiratory attainment of The Eighteen Arhan (a physical exercise which is condusive to health and body-strengthening suitable for both young and elder people);

The conventional skill of The Northern Shaolin Monastery for treatment in osteopathy; The study of relationship between the physiology function of the human body and position of caves in acupuncture.

The Secret of The Seven-Star Mantis Style is really a whole for reference of The Seven-Star Mantis Style in Chinese Matial Art.

1 November, 1985
LEE KAM WING MARTIAL ART SPORTS ASSOCIATION

Contents

Preface	4-5
Introduction of Shaolin Monastery	9-11
Founder of the Seven-Star Mantis Style and his Successors	12-15
About Grandmaster Chiu Chi Man	16-18
About Master Lee Kam Wing	19-49
Introduction of Seniority in the Kung Fu Family	50
The Seven-Star Mantis Style Give its Form	51-52
The Thirty-one Keywords Verbal Formula	53-76
The Eighteen Principle of Stances	77-86
The Thirteen Leg-Kicking Method	87-93
The Eighteen Palm Technique	94-101
The Junior Level of the Seven-Star Mantis Style Practising Series— The Pung Po	102-111
Explanation For Extracted Skills from the Pung Po Boxing Series	112-114
Method of Streching before Physical Strength Training	115-120
The Hand-to-Hand Combat	121-124
The Twenty-five Fist-fighting Technique	125-138
The Wooden Dummy Practising (Part I)	139-144

The Method of Wooden Dummy Practising (Part II)	145–147
The Method of Wooden Dummy Practising (Part III)	148–151
Method of Physical Strength Training	152–159

    1. Method of Dumbell
    2. Method of Rolling in Rigid Hand
    3. Method of Fingers-Scriping
    4. Method of Hand-rubbing
    5. The Hooked Hand practising in pair
    6. The Three-Star Hand and leg-kicking practising in pair
    7. The Rottan Ring practice
    8. The Tension Strength practice

The Essence of the Seven-Star Mantis Style	160–163

    1. The Spiritual Energy
    2. The Respiratory Force
    3. The Hands
    4. The Eyes
    5. The Body
    6. The Stance-Pacing
    7. The Principle Method of Offense in the Seven-Star Mantis Style
    8. The Striking Method of Keeping apart in Leg-Kicking
    9. The Method of Attacking while resisting
    10. The Method of Hand-Neglecting
    11. The Method of Mantis Pacing

The Analysis of Forces in the Seven-Star Mantis Style	164–166

    1. The Long Force
    2. The Short Force
    3. The Borrowed Force

The Intermediate Level of the Seven-Star Mantis Style Practising Series – The Black-Tiger-Cross	167–173
Explanation For Extracted From the Black-Tiger-Cross	174–177
The Advance Level of The Seven-Star Mantis Style Practising Series—The Mantis out of its Cave	178–191

Explanation For Extracted Skills From The Mantis
out of Its Cave   192–195

Method of Iron-Sand Palm Training   196–199
    1. The Sand Bag Method
    2. The Sand-inserting Method

The Conventional Chinese Medical prescription of Shaolin Monastery for Iron-Sand Palm Traning   200

The Application of Palm-fighting Technique   201–203

Domonstration for Weapons of the Seven-Star Mantis Style   204–206

The Sand Bag Practing   207–208

Principle for Prevention and Treatment of potential wound occured during Kung Fu practising   209–211
    1. Treatment of Muscular Infection
    2. Treatment of Muscular Cramp
    3. Treatment of Muscular Traumatisms
    4. Treatment of Dislocation of Shoulder Joint
    5. Treatment of Dislocation of Elbow Joint

Analysis and Application of the Vital point Striking and position of caves in Accupuncture   212–219

The Respiratory Attainment of the Eighteen Arhan   220–239

Introduction of the Shaolin Monastery

Chinese Martial Art has been in history for thousands of years. The Mantis Style is a kind of Chinese Martial Art (Chinese Kung Fu) originated from The Shaolin Monastery.

The Shaolin Monastery is situated among the enbrace of SONGSHAN (Mount Song) which is one of the so-called 'Five Greatest Mountains' in China. The Five Greatest Mountains (known as Wnyue 五嶽 in China are:-

   1. Taishan   (Mount Tai   泰山) in Shandong (山東)
   2. Huashan   (Mount Hua   華山) in Shaanxi   (江蘇)
   3. Songshan (Mount Song 嵩山) In Henan   (河南)
   4. Hengshan (Mount Heng 衡山) in Hunan   (湖南)
   5. Hengshan (Mount Heng 恒山) in Shanxi   (山西)

In the nineteenth year of the TAIHE Calendar (太和 i.e. 495 A.D.) of the Northern WEI (北魏) Dynasty, The emperor Xiaowen, whose own name was yuanhong (元宏), ordered to build the Shaolin Monastery to accommodate the Indian Monk Batuo (跋陀). Who came to SONGSHAN to preach Buddhism.

In the third year of XIAOCHANG Calendar (孝昌 i.e. 527 A.D.) The emperor was Xiaoming (孝明), Bodhidharma (known as Damo 達摩 in China) came to China from India to preach the Chan Buddhism (禪宗) in Shaolin Monastery. Thus he is recognized as the founder of Chinese Chan Buddhism, and the Shaolin Monastery is recognized as the ancestral home of the Chinese Chan Buddhism.

Many Monks in the Shaolin Monastery had already practised Martial Art before Bodhidharma came to China. In early TANG Dynasty (唐), Thirtheen Shaolin Buddists had saved the emperor's (TANG TAIZONG 唐太宗 -LI SHIMIN 李世民) life. The Shaolin Monastery got the emperor's comendation and awards. It then became famous over the whole country of China.

The legend was that the martial Art of The Shaolin Monastery was divided into thirty-six different FANGS (i.e. Rooms). Each FANG was specialized in some particular way of Kung Fu Technique. Nowaday, it is believed that they have been developed into different styles of Chinese Kung Fu.

The QUAN (boxing Series) 拳 套 of The Martial Art of The Shaolin Monerstery Martial Art are complex and forcefull. Their way of movements and performance are fierce and active and totally developing our abilities and force in self-defense or offense.

Founder of the Seven - Star Mantis Style and his Successors

FOUNDER OF THE SEVEN-STAR MANTIS STYLE

In Ming Dynasty (1368 A.D.), Wang Lang who is a Buddist of the Shaolin Monastery. One day, when he was sitting in the garden of the Monastery, he accidentally found that a cicada is firmly caught by a Mantis, although the cicada is more greater in size than the Mantis, the cicada was helplessly overwhelmed by the Mantis. As Wang Lang Watched the upright and stable body of the Mantis, and the two claws in its forearms is as rigid as a sickle, he was prompltly convinced that he picked up a reed stalk to brush at the Mantis. The Mantis immediately raised up its two rigid and speedy forearm and griped at the disturbing reed stalk.

Wang Lang was caught with interest using the reed stalk to brush at the Mantis from different direction, the principle of offense and self-defense and the spirit of brave-ahead of the Mantis makes Wang Lang calmed his mind to watch quietly and found that the brave and speedy force of the Mantis can be put into practice with the Chinese Martial Art.

Thereafter, Wang Lang caught plenty of the Mantis to observe the fighting technique of the Mantis during his spare time. The Mantis Style was then being generated by incorporating the foundation of Martial Art which Wang Lang had possessed beforehand. After being developed and spread rapidly with variation of different branch of the Mantis Style. It was interpreted that the Seven-Star Mantis Style is named from the brightness of the Big Dipper of the celestial phenomena, in which, the inside meaning is that disciples of the Seven-Star Mantis Style spread all over the world.

SUCCESSORS OF THE SEVEN-STAR MANTIS STYLE

WONG LANG (Founder) 　　　　　　　王朗（創派人）

1. SING SIL Master　　　　　　　　升霄
2. LEE SAN CHINE Master　　　　　李三剪
3. WONG WING SANG Master　　　王榮生
4. FANG YUK TOUNG Master　　　　范旭東
5. LOW KWANG YU Master　　　　　羅光玉
6. CHIU CHI MAN Master　　　　　　趙志民
7. LEE KAM WING Master　　　　　李錦榮

The mantis is catching the cicada

Worldwide Instructors:

Hong Kong	Instructor	Kwok Wing Ho
Hong Kong	Instructor	Au Chi Shing
Hong Kong	Instructor	Chan Sie Hung
Hong Kong	Instructor	Malcolm James Franklin
Hong Kong	Instructor	Alvin Law Wai Hon
Australia	Chief Instructor	Jimmy Tsui
Hungary	Chief Instructor	Richard Tix
England	Chief Instructor	Derek Frearson
Germany	Chief Instructor	Brunke Bast
Germany	Chief Instructor	Jörg Quade
United States	Chief Instructor	Jeffrey Bruflat
Italy Voghera	Chief Instructor	D'Aria Angelo
Italy Roma	Chief Instructor	Sergio Marzicchi
Italy Milan	Chief Instructor	Pierluigi Barrbieri
France	Instructor	Latouille Fabien
United States	Instructor	John Cheng M. D.
Ireland	Instructor	John O'Riordan
Germany	Instructor	Jochen Wolfgramm
Germany	Instructor	Nicolai Schild
Germany	Instructor	Marc Hübscher
Hungary	Instructor	Váradi Gyárgy
Hungary	Instructor	Kovács Lászlo
Hungary	Instructor	György Váraol
Italy	Instructor	Fabbricatore Pietro E Claudio

THE LATE GRANDMASTER LO KWANG YU
In the Chin Wu Athletic Association (The Mantis Catches the Cicada)

About Grandmaster Chiu Chi Man

Master Chiu Chi Man joined to learn the Northern Shaolin Martial Art from the Hong Kong Ching Wu Athletic Association in 1924.

In 1930, fifth successor of the Seven-Star Mantis Style, the late Grandmaster Lo Kwang Yu who was instructed by the Shanghai Ching Wu Athletic Association to offer tuition for the Seven-Star Mantis Style in the Hong Kong Ching Wu Athletic Association. Thereafter, Master Chiu Chi Man followed Grandmaster Lo Kwang Yu to study the Seven-Star Mantis Style.

Among, the four greatest style in the Shanghai Ching Wu Athletic Association are The Mantis Style, The Leg-deeping Style (The TAN TUI Style). The Eagle-claw Style and The Monkey Style. Grandmaster Lo Kwang Yu had been awarded a high respective rank for the Seven-Star Mantis Style in the Mantis Style.

In 1933, Master Chiu Chi Man was committed a position of Matial Art Supervisor for the Hong Kong Ching Wu Athletic Association and was confered by Grandmaster Lo Kwang Yu to act as an Assistant Instructor for the Seven-Star Mantis Style. Master Chiu was appointed to take over the tuition in teaching the Kung Fu lessons during Grandmaster Lo's absence for visiting outside the country for six years.

In 1938, Master Chiu and his Kung Fu brothers set up the Man Keung Althletic Association in Hong Kong. Master Chiu Chi Man was elected as the first chairman while Grandmaster Lo Kwang Yu was appointed as the Chief Instructor of the executive committee of the Association. Some time latter, the Pacific War was broken out, the Man Keung Athletic Association was forced to close down and Grandmaster Lo returned to his native place in Shang Tong Province.

In 1938

Master Lee Kam Wing receives the glorified flag from master Chiu Chi Man as a close-door disciple.

EXPLANATION FOR THE CHINESE COUPLET:

學得如山重 — The Limitation from our master is as great as the mountain.

承恩似海深 — The Spiritual Debt is as deep as the ocean.

About Master Lee Kam Wing

Master Lee Kam Wing who was born in Hong Kong, in 1947. Lee was introduced to master Chiu Chi Man by his maternal uncle while he was fifteen years old. He had spend ten years for learning the Seven-Star Mantis Style from Master Chiu Chi Man.

In 1972, Lee was encouraged by master Chiu Chi Man to set up his own Martial Art Association in Hong Kong in order to enhance and glorify The Seven-Star Mantis Style all over the world, Master Chiu Chi Man also passed 4 sets of the Seven-Star Mantis Style practising series and the practical medical prescription for treatment in osteopathy to Lee as a close door disciple.

Master Lee is now giving lessons of the Seven-Star Mantis Style to his students in Hong Kong and giving treatment in osteopathy for wounded people.

With a View to achieve an advanced medical experience in Chines osteopathy, he had been completed a Chinese medical course in Acupunture in the Zhaoqing Medical School in Zhaoqing City in China, and also, he had been finished an advanced course in studying the Chinese osteopathy from Doctor Ng Chung Lung who is a graduate from the most famous Fat Shan Orthopaedics Hospital in the Fat Shan City in China.

In order to put the real contact of fighting technique of the Seven-Star Mantis Style into practice, Master Lee gives practical training to his students for attending a Free-fighting Completion which is being held frequently in Hong Kong.

Beside Master Lee is a Sincere Buddhist. Since 1981, he had been studying the Buddism under Master Kwok Kong who is now the principle of the Hong Kong Buddhism Association.

In November 1985, Master Lee Kam Wing was in invited as an instructor of the Hong Kong Ching Wu Athletic Association for giving lessons on Seven-Star Mantis Style.

The posture of sifu Siu Chyi-Lin (Unicorn Chan)

Siu Chyi-Lin (Unicorn Chan) gave a photo to Lee Kam Wing for memory, besides Siu Chyi Lin was the super star, Lee Siu-Lung.

20

Ching Wu Association
Chair man 廖國存
Lui Kwok Chuen

Ching Wu Association
President 郭培佳 Kwok Pui Kai

Ching Wu Association
Wing Tsun
蔡鎮全 Sifu Choi Chun Chuen

鐵虎門歐雄彪 Sifu
Iron Tiger Style
Sifu Au Hung Bill

To Sifu Lee Kam Wing,
from British Taijiquan
and Shaolin Kung Fu Association.
Sifu Derek Frearson

To Sifu Lee Kam Wing,
from Rao Rao Zhao, China.

蔡李佛羅祺師傅崔廣源師傅合照
Choi Lee Fat
Sifu Law Kei
and Sifu Tsui Kown Yuen

朱家螳螂鄭運師傅
詠春李潤添師傅
Chu Kar Mantis
Sifu Cheng Rung
Wing Tsun
Sifu Lee Yun Tim

Ching Wu Association Member
鐵虎門歐國誠 Sifu
Iron Tiger Style
Sifu Au Kwok Shing

李錦榮師傅吾兄出兩版誌慶

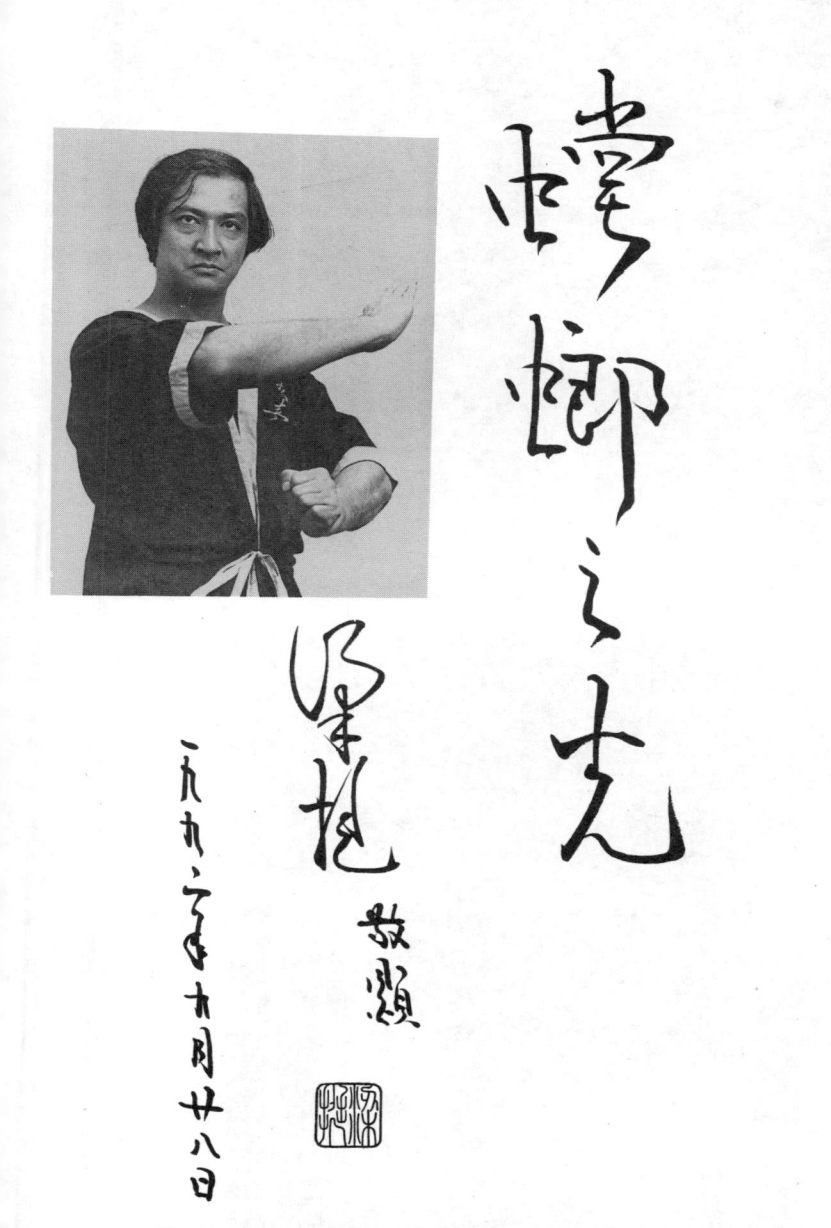

螳螂之光

梁挺 敬題

一九九二年十月廿八日

To Sifu Lee Kam Wing, author of the Secret of Seven-Star Mantis Style. from Leung Ting.

98, U.S.A. Houston Seminar

Jeffrey J. Bruflat, John Cheng M.D.
Grand Master Chiu Chi Man, Master Lee Kam Wing

Kungfu Brother: CHIU LUEN - U.S.A.

Adopted Son
William Lapham.
U.S.A.

25

Master Lee Kam Wing and Master Chan Chun Shan and Master Lee Koon Hung

The Movie Star of TBS in Japan graduated and received certificate by Master Lee Kam Wing

Guang Zhow Ching Wu Atheltic Association.
Appointed Master Lee Kam Wing to be consultant.

Guang Zhow Ching Wu
Wing Tsun Style Master Yun Jo Tong

Hong Kong Taiji Mantis Style
Master Kwong Kwen Wai, 1991

1985, The Janpan Students, 1985.

Master Lee Kam Wing took a photo with the Choi Mok Style sifu Lau Bill in 1978

May 1996, Master Lee Kam Wing, with England: Derek Frearson,
Hungary: Richard Tix, Italy: Voghera, Angelo Dària, Rome: Sergio Màrzicchi,
Milano: Pierluigi Barbieri, All instructor in Italy Seminary.

97年7月香港回歸中國
世界精武會大匯演合照
Hong Kong Changeover to China
World Chin Woo Demonstration

97年7月香港回歸中國
世界精武大匯演合照
Hong Kong Changeover to China
World Chin Woo Demonstration

八卦掌李小雲師傅
廣州詠春馮銳堅師傅
精武會主席郭培佳
Ba Qua Chang Sifu Lee Siu Wan
Guang Zhou Wing Tsun Sifu Fung Yu Kin
President Kwok Pui Kai

太極拳陳金英師傅
Tai Chi Chuan Sifu Chan Kam Ying

Master Lee Kam Wing
Grand Master Chiu Chi Man
Master Ruc Chung
Master Jimmy Tsui

鷹爪派林永傑師傅
精武會會長廖國存
Eagle Claw
Sifu Lam Wing Kit

29

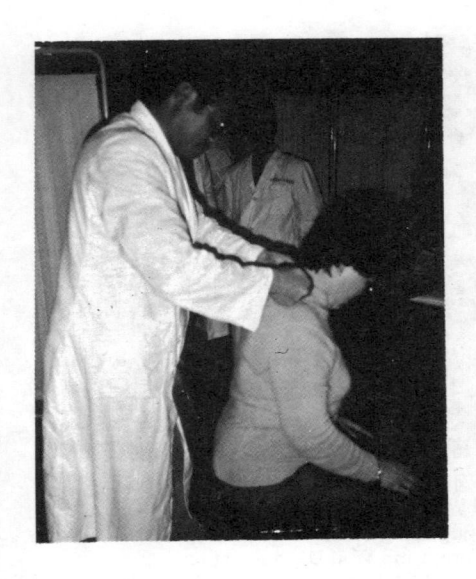

Master Lee Kam Wing pursued advanced study in Canton

The teacher of acupuncture and moxibustion in Canton

The Lion dance demonstration in Canton

Master Lee Kam Wing gave a Golrified Flag to the honorary president, Chan Siu Pang.

Left Side Frank Scholz
Right Side Chief Instructor Brunke Bast.

31

匈牙利 Richard Tix Chief Instructor

Chinese Marital Art Association Sifu Lee Kwun Hung, Sifu Chan Sau Chong, Sifu Lua Chi Keung, Sifu Cheung Tin Hung, ect ....

Kung-Fu-Nachwuchs fährt zur EM

Seven-Star Mantis in Germany the students got the second, forth, fifth prizes in the International Kung Fu Competition on 30th May 1985

1998年 26 Anniversary

Sifu Lee Kam Wing Student got the first prize in Hong Kong Martial Art Competition

The Iron-dummy demonstration

34

Sifu Lee Kam Wing in 1985

The opening ceremony of the Police Station in Choi Hung Estate Kowloon.

Oct, 1994. Master Lee Kam Wing, The Seminary in England.

Madam Yang Lei Hsien The popularly elected Councillor of the Urban Council.

The Movie star of TBS in Japan came to Hong Kong to learn the Seven Star Martial Arts Kung Fu by Lee Kam Wing, on November 1984.

Master Lee Kum Wing took a photo in Martial Art Association's demonstration room in 1984.

37

Master Lee Kam Wing in Kwun Chung Temple in Fanling (1983)

Master Lee and Master KWOK KONG the Chairman of Hong Kong Buddism Association in 1981.

Master Lee Kam Wing and Graduates of the Hong Kong Buddism Association.

May 1996, Master Lee Kam Wing with Angelo Dària, Sergio Marzicchi and Pierluigi Barbieri. Italy instructors visit Pa Kwa Style Sifu Michele Rubino.

The Lion Dance Demonstration in ATV Hong Kong.

In 1983, by Hong Kong Television Broadcasting Co. Ltd.,

The Demonstration of Lion Dance in ATV

Prizes

The student of Master Lee Kam Wing won two free contact in June and September in 1984.

The photo of Grandmaster Chiu Chi Man and Sifu Lee Kam Wing in 1970.

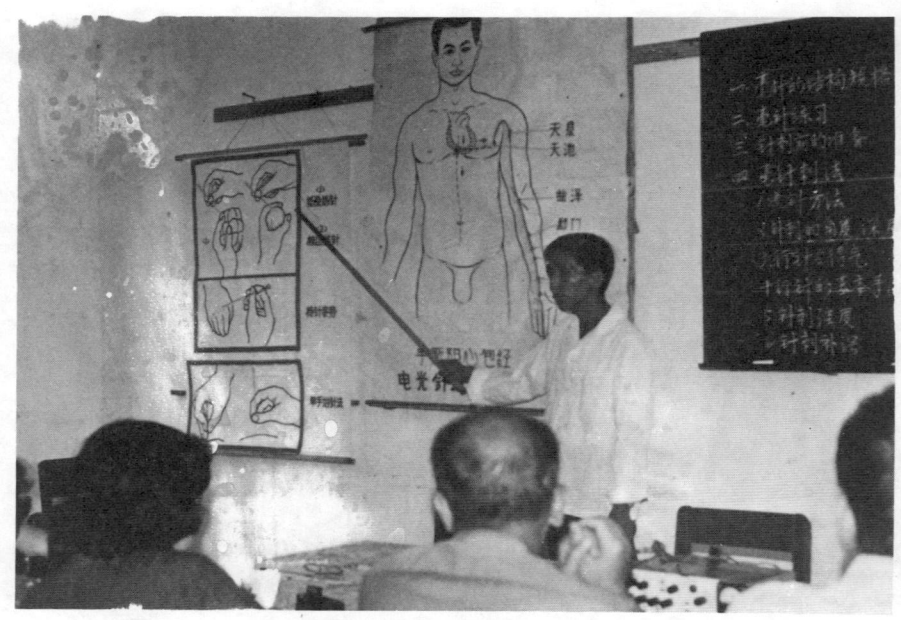

The Sanitation school in Canton.

Master Lee Kam Wing was graduate from College of Traditional Chinese Medicine.

Inspector of Kowloon Police Headquarter gives Eyes-Lightening for the awakened Lion in 1982.

Left: Master Lee Chau, The President of Pak Mei Style Kwok Chang Martial Art Association.
Middle: Master Chan Hon Chung, The President of Hong Kong Chinese Martial Art Association
Right: Master Lee Kam Wing

The Eleventh Anniversary of Master Lee's Association in 1983.

Same above

44

A social gathering with the Shamshuipo Police Headquarter in 1980.

Master Chan Shiu Chung of The Monkey Style and Master Lee Kam Wing.

45

Master Chiu Chun Tak of Shan Chien Do Institute from Singapore and Master Lee Kam Wing

1995, 23 ANNIVERSARY.

Instructor Alan Smith & Chief Instructor Derek Frearson in England Seminar.

John Cheng M.D.
Master Lee Kam Wing
Malcolm James Frenklin
Jeffrey J. Bruflat

Instructor John O'Riordan Irish Republic Ireland

佛山精武會區榮鉅
Fut San Chin Woo
Sifu Au Wing Gui

1994 Master Lee Kam Wing and Derek Frearson, Lady Mayoress, Mrs. Jasqueline Robinson, Maurice Chan, Mr. Russell, Simon and Lord Mayor, Mrs. Margaret Bell.

山東七星螳螂鍾連寶師傅
梅花螳螂危鳳池師傅合照
Shan Tung Mantis
Sifu Zhong Lian Bao
Mui Fa Mantis
Sifu Ai Fung Chi

空手道柯智瀧師傅
迷宗羅漢余長江師傅
副主席蕭鎮昇
Karate Sifu Ou Chun Lung
My Jhong Law Horn
Sifu Yu Cheung Kwon
Vice President Siu Chung Sing

刨花蓮詠春
文子超師傅
Pao Fa Lien Wing Chun
Sifu Man Tze Chiu

霍元甲（精武會創始者）遺像
Founder of The Ching Wu Athletic Association
Master HUOH YUAN CHIA

Introduction of Seniority in the Kung Fu Family

1. JO-SI   祖師   (Founder of a Style)
2. CHUNG-SI   宗師   (Grandmaster of a Style)
3. SI-PAK   師伯   (Elder Kung Fu Brother of Si-Fu)
4. SI-SOAK   師叔   (Younger Kung Fu brother of Si-Fu)
5. SI-FU   師父   (Kung Fu Instructor)
6. MOON-TO   門徒   (Disciple)
7. DAI-GEE   弟子   (Student)
8. SI-HING   師兄   (Elder Kung Fu Brother)
9. SI-JE   師姐   (Elder Kung Fu Sister)
10. SI-DEI   師弟   (Younger Kung Fu Brother)
11. SI-MUI   師妹   (Younger Kung Fu Sister)

The Seven - Star Mantis Style Gives Its Form

Since plenty of Seven-Star Mantis Boxing Series have been offered a whole development in training flexible variation of joints in the human body and enhancing the respiratory strength in physical training, a prompt reaction can be reached while one in facing a real contact in fighting.

Although many of the Boxing Series had been greatly created, however the application of skills among the Boxing Series are being simply realised and put in practice.

There must be a basic principle for any kind of the Kung Fu Style; as if there will not be a way for taking a good Kung Fu practice where an unique form is not being created.

The Seven-Star Mantis Style is a kind of Northern Martial Art in Chinese, which is fierce, speedy and moving actively with the corporation of rigidness and smoothness. The rigid pair of clawed forearm of the mantis can catch creatures, besides, it can also capture a bigger and stronger in size of Chameleon than itself. Generally, it can be heard of a "pickpark" sound from the Seven Star Mantis Style as fist is being punched during Kung Fu practice. The aim is to create an elastic strength in skins of the forearms following a long period of hard training. The act of the Seven-Star Mantis Style is stably fast and simply purified. It becomes real while it is considered as false, it becomes false while it is considered as real.

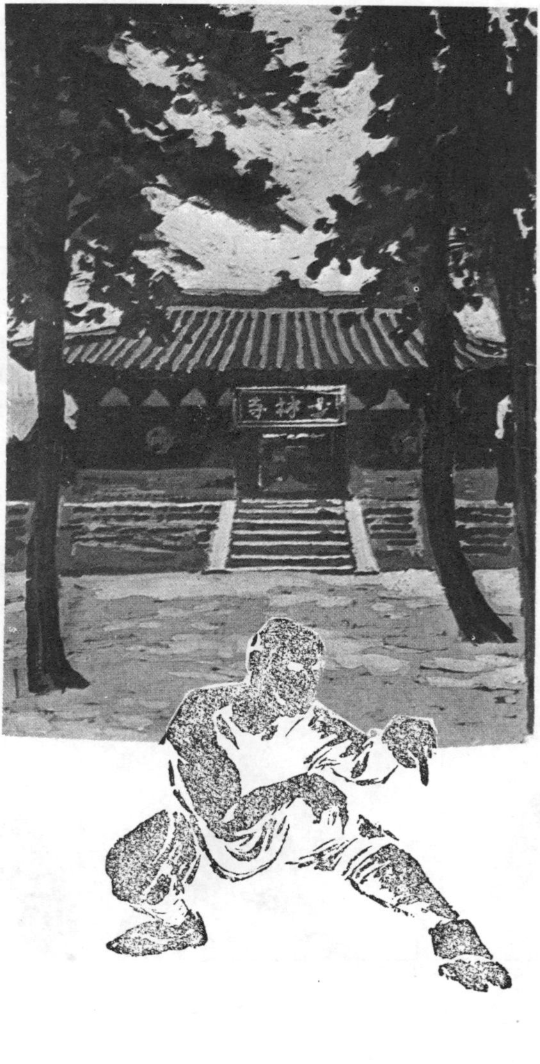
少林寺

The Thirty - one Keywords Verbal Formula

1. **OU (Hook)** 拘
   The Movement in this skill which incorporated a sideway push after griping up the coming attack from an oponent is named as False-Hand (figure 1-7)

2. LOU (Grapple) 摟

The word LOU in Chinese is to mean something which is being catched. When this skill is appled together with the skill OU (Hook) as a method of subsidiary it becomes a Real-Hand. (figure 8-14)

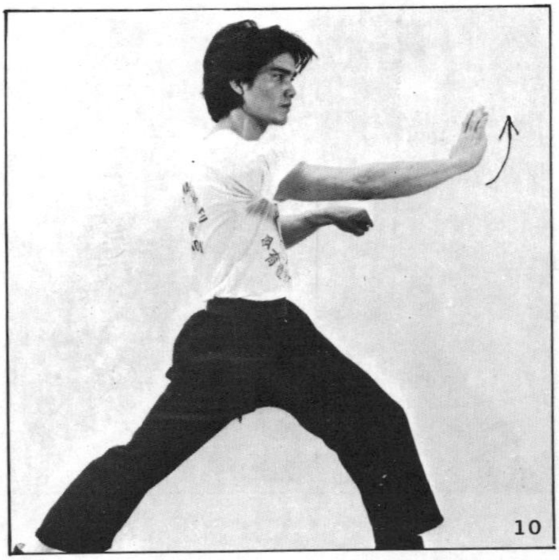
10

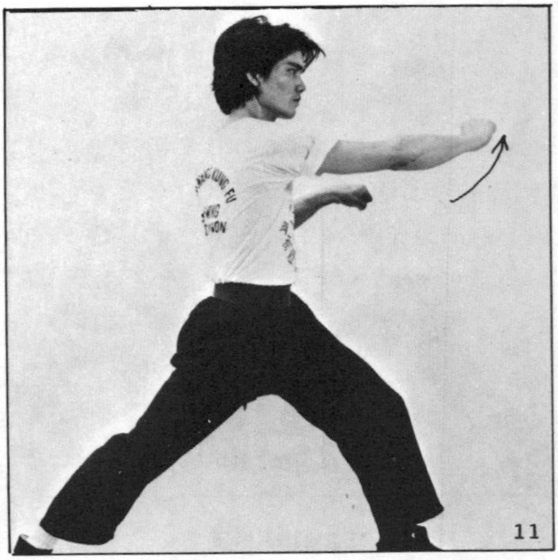
11

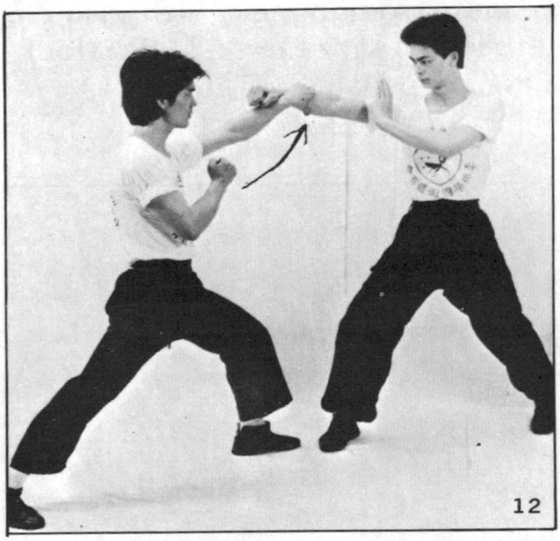
12

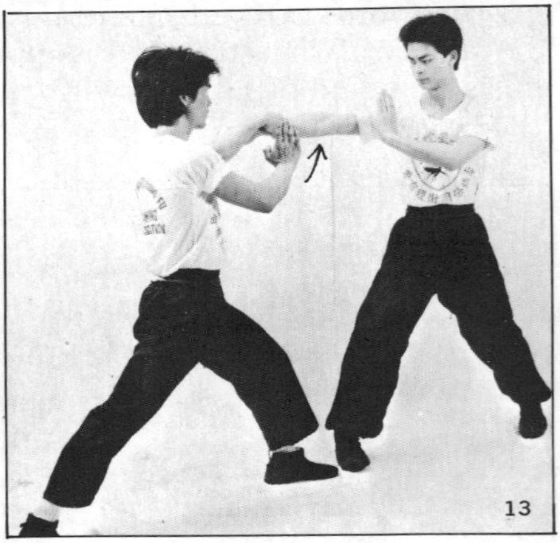
13

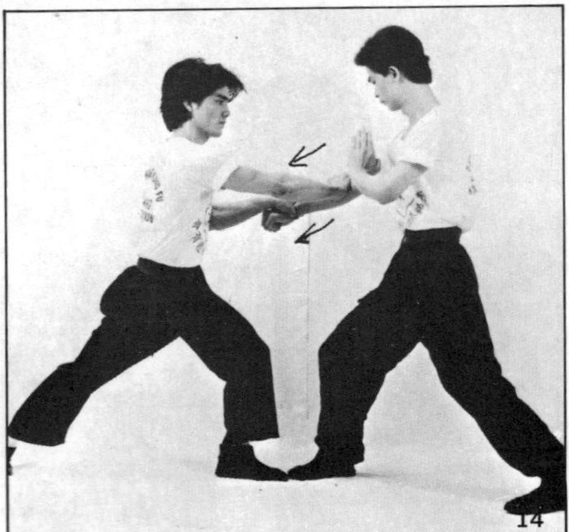
14

3. **TSAI (Pluk)** 採

The importance of this skill is to incorporate both the skill Hook and Grapple into a hand-plucking skill which can sucessefully make an invisible skill. As the application of both Hook and Grapple can cause the opponent fall down toward the front, which is similary like an action in plucking down fruites from the tree. It becomes a Hand-plucking when another punch is added to strike at the opponent (figure 15-16)

15

16

4. **KWA (Block)** 掛

The word KWA in Chinese is meant to hang up something from lower to upper point (figure 17-20)

17

19

57

5. **TIAO (Intercept)** 刀
   The act of the skill TIAO is to close tightly the last three fingers, while the thumb and the index finger are hold together to make a hook in a form of keenness and activity. (figure 21-27)

6. **PENG (Chop)** 崩

The movement of the skill PENG is to mean a forceful fist heavely chopping downward from the above head with a tendency of mountain—collapsing (figure 28-34)

59

7. CHAN (Contact) 粘
A reliable but tough skill in contacting the coming attack. (figure 35-37)

60

8. **NIEN (Cling)** 黏
   The skill NIEN is generally applied together with the skill CHAN as clammy as paint to stick the coming attack. (figure 38-39)

9. **TIEH (Tag)** 貼
   The word TIEH in Chinese is meant to get a close attack with the opponent. (figure 40-41)

10. KAO (Lean) 靠

The skill KAO is generally applied together with the skill TIEH when this two skills are put together into application, it becomes a close contact in attacking. (figure 42-43)

11. SHAN (Dodge) 閃

The word SHAN in Chinese is meant to escape and avoid the coming attack. (figure 44-47)

12. TENG-NUO (Bounce) 騰挪
The skill TENG-NUO is generally applied for a quick movement in a close contact. Which incorporate a skillful Leg-kicking technique. (figure 48-51)

63

13. **TSO (Dent)** 挫
The application of this skill is to punch diagonally from below to above. (figure 52-58)

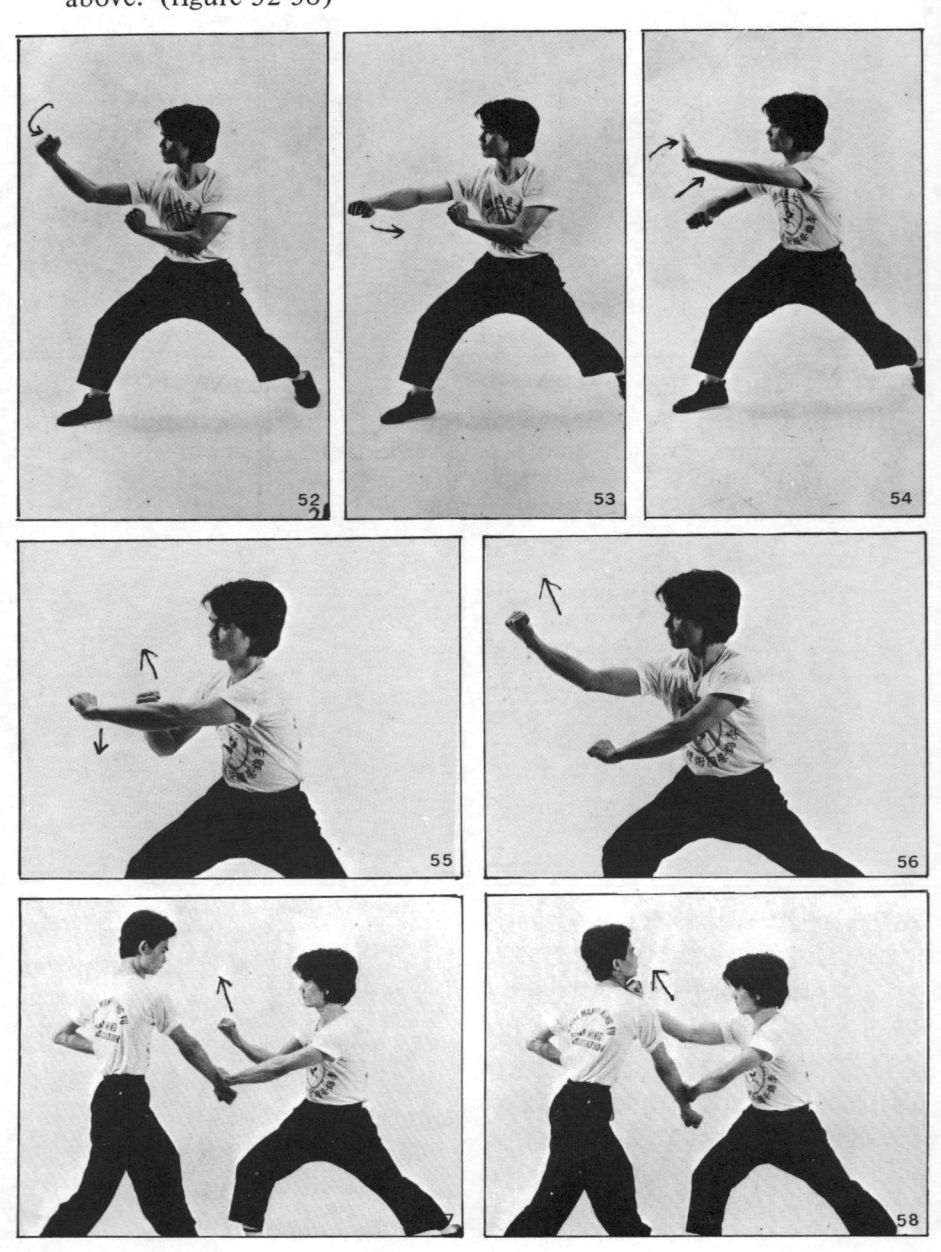

64

14. TUNG (Straight Forward) 統
The act of the skill TUNG is to launch a fierce attack without fear, it belongs to a skill of Vehemence. (figure 59-63)

15. TIAO (Ward off) 挑
The skill TIAO is meant to sprout from below to above. (figure 64-69)

65

64
65
66
67
68
69

16. FENG (Grasp) 封
The skill FENG is meant to close up the coming attack from inside to outside or from inside to outside. (figure 70-71)

17. PU (Supplement) 補
The skill PU is meant to add for the situation. (figure 72-73)

67

18. CHUAN (Circle) 圈

The skill CHUAN is meant to give a round about striking at the opponent's unguarded part. (figure 74-75)

19. SHIH-PI (Powerful chop) 勢劈

The skill SHIH-PI is to mean a tendency of chopping downward with powerful force. (figure 76-79)

20. **CHAN (Wrap)** 纏

A useful skill of hand to hand control, which can clutch tightly and makes the opponent no way to escape. (figure 80-83)

69

21. TOU (Filch) 偷
The skill TOU is to attack surprisingly at the opponent's unwarned part. (figure 84-87)

84

85

86

87

22. LAU (Slip) 漏
A skillful striking method in between the opponent's ungaurded attacking area. (figure 88-92)

88

89

90

91

92

71

23. **FAN (Flutter)** 翻
    A kind of hand-revolving skill similar to a movement of scoop wheel. figure 93-97)

24. **TING (Prop)** 頂
    A short of fierce attack generally applied in close distance contact. (figure 98-99)

25. PONG (Topple) 榜

The skill PONG is the application of hand-bumping which can cause the opponent loss his balance in a close contact. (figure 100-101)

73

26. TSU (Sieze) 捽
A unique skill of weakening the opponent's coming attack. (figure 102-103)

27. LU (Strike) 捋
The skill LU is to press down the attacking arm at the opponent's elbow joint. (figure 104-105)

28. TI (Hang) 提
An upward Leg-hanging skill which is commonly acted as a method of defense while in attack. (figure 106-107)

29. TAN (Spring) 彈
An elastic skill of expanding and contracting the fingers front and back. (figure 108-110)

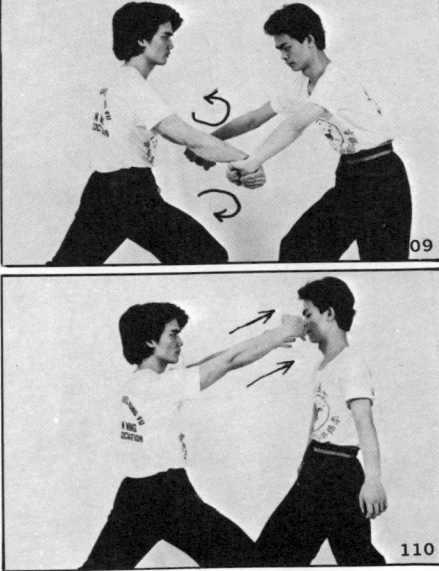

75

30. **TO (Cast off)** 脫

The skill TO is meant to get free by skimming off the opponent control. (figure 111-114)

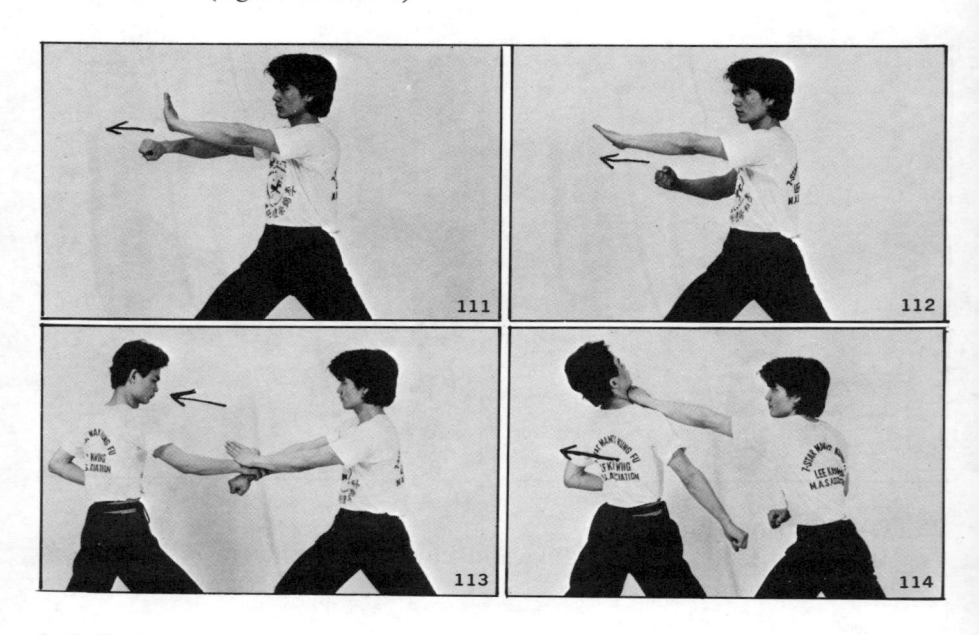

31. CHIU (Sprout) 揪
A skillful Leg-kicking method of kicking upward at the lower part of the opponent. This skill is generally applied together with a help of Hand-striking at the upper part of the opponent. (figure 115-116)

The Eighteen Principle of Stances

THE SEVEN-STAR STANCE (七星步)
Among Stances of Seven-Star Mantis Style, the Seven-Star Stance has the influence which can draw and release freely. For thus, there must a Seven-Star Stance be included in most of the Seven-Star Mantis Style practising series. (figure 117-118)

THE CIRCLE ENTERING STANCE (入環步)
The principle strenght of the Circle Entering Stance is concentrated in the rear bended leg.
(figure 119-120) the practioner bends his left leg to lower his body, while he bends his right knee by the side of the ankle of the left leg, so as to punch at the lower unguarded part of the opponent.

THE MONKEY STANCE (猿猴步)
The Monkey Stance also named as the Medium Stance (中式) the act of the Monkey Stance is to bend slightly both knees of the leg. (figure 121-122)

THE FILCHING STANCE (偷步)
The movement of the Filching Stance is to place horizontally one step behind another leg to get closely into the opponent's inner space. (figure 123-124)

THE TIGER-RIDING STANCE (跨虎步)
The Tiger-Riding Stance is to bend the knee of the rear leg, while the front leg is bent to lift the heel with the point of the foot rest on ground (figure 125-126)

THE COLLAPSING STANCE (吞蹋步)
The Collapsing Stance also named as the Reverse Hill-climbing Stance (反弓式) The act of the Collapsing Stance is to bend the knee of the rear leg vertically, while the front leg is stretched sloppingly toward the front. (figure 127-128)

127

128

THE MOUSE STANCE (鼠步)
The Mouse Stance also named as the False Stance (虛式), The posture of the Mouse Stance is to lean the upper part of the body sloppingly ahead, while the knee of the rear leg is bend to concentrat the principle strenght and the front leg is stretched straightly in align with the rear foot. (figure 129-130)

129

130

THE LEG-BOUNCING STANCE (蹤步)
The objective of the Leg-Bouncing is to draw the distance close with the opponent, the act of the Stance is to strike with the knee of the front leg at the middle part of the opponent by tracing up the rear leg in front, while the knee of the front leg is bounced upward. (figure 131-132)

81

THE HILL-CLIMBING STANCE (登山馬)
The Hill-Climbing Stance also named as the Bow Stance (弓箭馬), the act of the Stance is to bend the knee of the front leg making the outer face of the knee in align with the point of the foot. (figure 133-134)

THE HORSE-RIDING STANCE (騎馬式)
The Horse-Ring Stance also named as the Four-Stabling Stance, The point of the Stance is that distance between the bend legs should not keeping too much apart from each other, but a natural manner for lowering the straight body is essential. (figure 135-136)

THE LEG-HANGING STANCE (提馬)
The act of the Leg-Hanging Stance is to lift the front leg up to the belly height while the raised foot is pointing downward. (figure 137-138)

THE BACK-KICKING STANCE (背踢馬)
The use of the Back-Kicking Stance is to bump a horizontal kick at a lower level from the rear of the knee joint of the front leg while the front leg is bend slightly to concentrate the center weight of the body (figure 139-140)

139

140

THE CROSS STANCE (十字馬)
The principle of the Cross Stance is to kick straightly ahead at middle level of an opponent while another leg is slightly bend to stable the body. (figure 141-142)

141

142

THE TOPPLING STANCE (蹬扑式)
The act of the Toppling Stance is first to advance the left leg one step behind the right leg and then to prop the stretched right leg backward along a curved direction in front. (figure 143-144)

THE CROSS-LEG STANCE (扭馬)
The movement of the Cross-Leg Stance is to twist both of the legs from left to right while the stance is retained in a original position. (figure 145-146)

THE PROPING STANCE (扑腿)
The point of the Proping Stance is first to turn the body backward from right to left, and then to prop the stretched front leg ahead, while the rear leg is bent to lower the body. (figure 147-148)

147

148

THE ATTENTION STANCE (叠步)
The use of the Attention Stance is to hold the rear leg together with the front leg in front, so as to draw close the distance with the opponent. (figure 149-151)

149

150

151

THE WITHDRAW STANCE (撤步)
The objective of the Withdraw Stance is to draw the rear leg backward while the front leg is setting back accordinly. So as to draw away the distance with the opponent. (figure 152-154)

152   153   154

The Thirteen Leg - kicking Method

THE LEG-BUMPING KICK 扎腿
Figure (155-156) shows The Boxer bumps with the forced horizontal foot of his rear leg at the opponent's kneecap or shinbone.

THE LEG-SPROUTING KICK 揪腿
Figure (157-158) shows the Boxer kicks horizontally upward from rear of the lower part of the opponent's leg.

THE LEG-PROPPING KICK 扑腿
The act of the Leg-Proping Kick is first to raise up one leg in front and then at the same time to turn aside the body while proping out another leg from rear at the opponent's kneecap. (figure 159-160)

THE DOOR-SHUTTERING KICK 閉門腿
The Door-Shuttering Kick also named as the Groin Kick which is dangerously used for kicking at the lower important point of the opponent. (figure 161-162)

THE WHIRLWIND KICK 旋風腿
The Whirlwind Kick also named as the Frontier Kick (前空月腿).
the act of the Whirlwind Kick is to kick aside rapidly a stretched leg at the upper part of the opponent, while the legs is off ground (figure 163-164)

THE LEG-SQUATING KICK 掃堂腿
The use of the Leg-Squating Kick is to to squat around the stretched leg while the hands prop on ground. (figure 165-166)

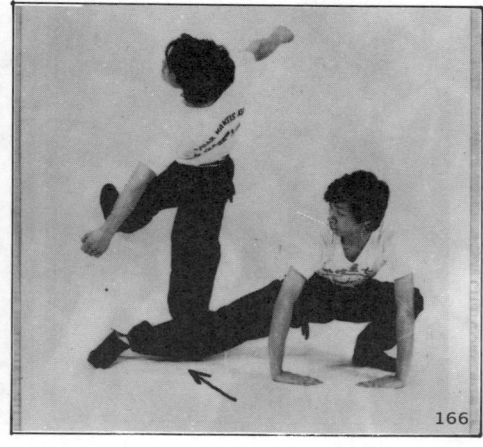

THE LOTUS LAYOUT KICK 擺蓮腿
The method of the Layout Kick is to sweep a stretched leg upward from a reverse direction at the upper part of the opponent. (figure 167-168)

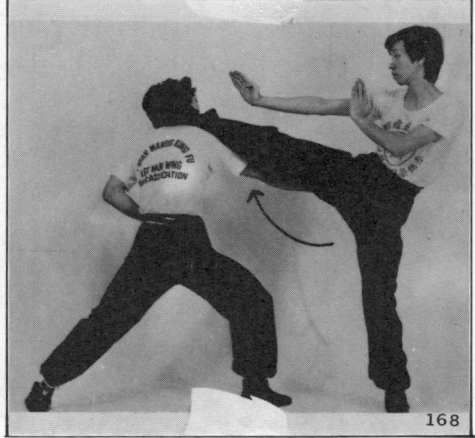

THE SINGLE LEG-SOARING KICK 單飛腿
The objective of the Single Leg-Soaring Kick is to give a pierce kick at the upper level of the opponent with the act of bumping a forced leg from rear while the body is jumping ahead. (figure 169-170)

THE CROSS KICK 十字腿

The use of the Cross Kick is to apply both the Groin Kick and the thursting Palm at the same time, while the opponent's hand is being grappled. (figure 171-172)

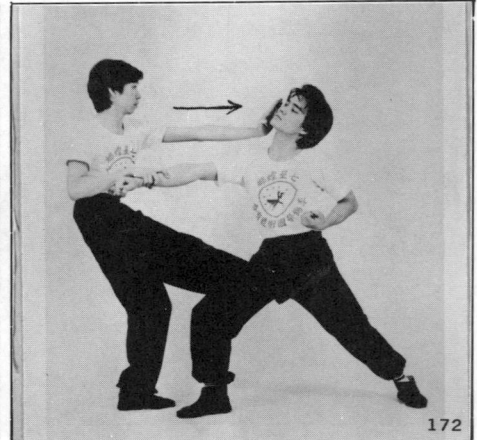

THE SPRING-FILCHING KICK 偷彈腿

The use of the Spring-Filching Kick is to spring the forced front leg backward at the rear of the opponent's front leg, so as to loss the opponent's balance. (figure 173-176)

173

174

175

176

THE CHEST-PIERCING KICK 穿心腿
The Chest-Piercing Kick is a kind of fiercing Leg-Kicking method which is to bump the powerful leg straight ahead at the opponent's front chest. (figure 177-178)

177

THE TOPPLING KICK WITH FILCHING STANCE 偷步蹬扑腿
The act of the Toppling Kick is first to place one step behind the front leg, so as to enter the front leg along a curved direction into the rear of the opponent's leg and cause the opponent loss his balance. (figure 179-180)

THE UPWARD BLOCK BUMPING KICK 掛撐腿
The use of the Upward Block Bumping Kick is to apply both the Chest-piercing and thrusting palm at the same time, while the opponent's coming attack is being resisted at the upper level (figure 181-182)

The Eighteen Palm Technique

THE POSITIVE AND NEGATIVE PALM 陰陽掌
The Positive and Negative Palm also named as The Double Dispeling Palm which is to push aside both stretched palms from left to right. (figure 183-184)

THE HALTING PALM 封掌
The Halting Palm is meant to push an upturned thrusting palm ahead, while the coming attack is being halted by another hand at a lower level. (figure 185-186)

THE REVERSE PALM 反面掌
The act of the Reverse Palm is to repress downward with the back of the palm after withdrawing it back from the front area, while the coming attack is being halted by another hand. (figure 187-188)

THE SLIP-ROLLING PALM 滾漏掌
The act of the Slip-Rolling Palm is to re-circle the front palm from left to right after withdrawing it back from the front area. (figure 189-191)

THE PROPPING PALM 頂掌
The objective of the Propping Palm is to prop ahead a horizontal thrusting palm, while the coming attack is being grappled at above head. (figure 192-193)

THE FILING PALM 挫掌
The act of the Filing Palm is to push upward a stretched palm in front while the coming attack is being grappled by another hand at upper level. (figure 194-195)

THE FILCHING PALM 偷掌
The Filiching Palm is meant to push ahead quickly an invisible stretched palm after pressing down the coming attack from left and right respectively. (figure 196-198)

THE BRUSHING PALM 挑掌
The act of the Brushing Palm is to circle upward both the front and rear upturned palm from left to right. (figure 199-200)

THE WAIST-CHOPPING PALM 斬腰掌
The application of the Waist-Chopping Palm is to force a stretched palm at the opponent's waist height, as the coming attack is being grappled down by another hand. (figure 201-202)

THE UPWARD BLOCK THRUSTING PALM 掛面掌
The act of the Upward Block Thursting Palm is push ahead an upturned fiercing palm, as the coming attack is being block at above head by another hand. (figure 203-204)

THE ROUND HOUSE PALM 圈掌
The skill of the Round House Palm is to circle upward the forearm in front from left to right. (figure 205-207)

99

THE PLUM BLOSSOM PALM 梅花掌
The act of the Plum Blossom Palm is to circle both the palms from left to right in front so as to push the unwarned stretching palm ahead. (figure 208-210)

THE DOUBLE PRESSING PALM 雙壓掌
The use of the Double Pressing Palm is to push ahead both of the upturned thrusting palm with a circle entering stance. (figure 211-212)

THE CHIPPING PALM 撇掌
The act of the chipping palm is to push ahead a stretched horizontal palm, while the stretched palm is facing upward. (figure 213-214)

THE DOUBLE DOOR PALM 雙門掌
To spring ahead both thursting palm after holding back the Double palms in front. (figure 215-216)

THE OVERWHELMING PALM 翻天印掌
First, the boxer press down the coming attack with the right hand at below and the left hand at above with a leg-hanging stance, at the same time he overturns the stretched left hand down in front. (figure 217-219)

THE THRUSTING PALM 插掌
The boxer push aside the coming attack while he forces an upturned left palm ahead. (figure 220-221)

THE MILLSTONE PALM 磨盆掌
Figure (222-224) shows the Boxer circle both of his hands in front while he pushes his right palm ahead upwardly.

102

The Junior Level of the Seven - Star Mantis Style practising Series - The PUNG PO

1. The Supplementary Fist with Tiger-Riding Stance   figure 454—458
   跨虎步補捶
2. The Mantis catches the cicada   figure 459
   螳螂捕蟬
3. The Left Thrusting Palm with Attention Stance   figure 460—461
   叠步捶拳
4. The Supplementary Fist with right Hill-Climbing Stance   figure 462
   進右登山補捶
5. The Grappling punch with Leg-Bouncing Stance   figure 463
   縱步封統捶
6. The right Elbow-Striking with Circle-Entering Stance   figure 464
   入環步右叠肘
7. The right Back Chopping Fist with Circle-Entering Stance   figure 465
   入環步右崩捶
8. The Rear Treasure-Plucking.   figure 466
   背後探寶
9. The Grappling Hand with Horse Riding Stance   figure 467
   馬式封手
10. The left Intercepted Hand with Hill-Climbing Stance.   figure 468
    登山左刁手
11. The right Chopping Fist with Hill-Climbing Stance.   figure 469
    登山右劈捶
12. The Hook Grapple and Pluck with Hill-Climbing Stance.   figure 470
    登山拘摟探手
13. The Little Scoop Wheel Fist with Tiger-Riding Stance. (The Pung Po Fist) 跨虎小翻車   figure 471
14. The left Thrusting Palm with Hill-Climbing Stance After Attention Stance. figure 472—473
    叠步登山左插掌

103

15. The Supplementary Fist with right Hill-Climbing Stance.　figure 474
　　進右登山補捶
16. The double grappling hands with Horse-Riding Stance.　figure 475
　　右後退馬式雙封手
17. The Waist-Chopping Palm with left Hill-Climbing Stance after Attention Stance.　figure 476
　　叠步左登山斬腰掌
18. The left Back Chopping Punch with Horse-Riding Stance.　figure 477
　　馬式左崩捶
19. The downward Intercepted Hand with Leg-hanging Stance.
　　提馬下刁手　figure 478
20. The upward Intercept Hand with Leg-hanging Stance.　figure 479
　　提馬反提刁
21. The Chopping Fist with right Horse-Riding Stance.　figure 480
　　進右馬劈捶
22. The right upward Elbow with Cross-Leg Stance.　figure 481
　　扭馬右拐肘
23. The right thursting palm with left Hill-Climbing Stance.　figure 482
　　左上登山右插掌
24. The left Supplementary Fist with Horse-Riding Stance.
　　馬式左補捶　figure 483
25. The Seven-Star left Leg-Sprouting Kick.　figure 484
　　七星左揪腿
26. The Seven-Star right Leg-Sprouting Kick.　figure 485
　　七星右揪腿
27. The Mantis Catches the Cicada.　figure 486
　　螳螂捕蟬
28. The Eyes-Plucking with Door-Shuttering Kick.　figure 487
　　探腿撩陰腿
29. The Palm-Shearing and the Mantis spies cave　figure 488—489
　　剪掌螳螂探洞
30. The right Round House Punch with Attention Stance.　figure 490
　　合步右圈捶
31. The downward Block with Leg-Hanging Stance.　figure 491
　　提腿下截手
32. The upward Ward Off Fist with Leg-hang Stance　figure 492
　　提腿上挑捶
33. The Waist-Chopping palm with Grappling Hand.　figure 493
　　封手斬腰掌
34. The left Counter-Intercept Hand.　figure 494
　　纏絲左措捶

35. The right Counter-Intercept Hand. figure 495
    纏絲右措捶
36. The Upward Block and Navel-Proping Punch. figure 496
    掛手頂臍捶
37. The Hand-Faning with right Collapsing Stance. figure 497
    進右吞蹋扇風手
38. The Hand-Faning with left Collapsing Stance after turning backward by the left. figure 498
    後轉左吞蹋扇風手
39. The Hand-Faning with right Collapsing Stance. figure 499
    進右吞蹋風手
40. The Waist-Chopping With left Seven-Star Stance. figure 500
    七星引針斬腰
41. The left Round House Punch with Hill-Climbing Stance. figure 501
    登山左圈捶
42. The left Back Chopping Fist with Hill-Climbing Stance. figure 502
    登山左崩捶
43. The Seven-Star left Intercepted Hand. figure 503
    七星左刁手
44. The Seven-Star right supplementary punch. figure 504
    七星右補捶
45. The Mantis catches the Cicada after turning backward by the left.
    左轉後螳螂捕蟬 figure 505—508

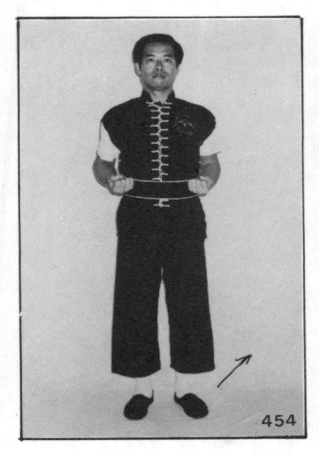

105

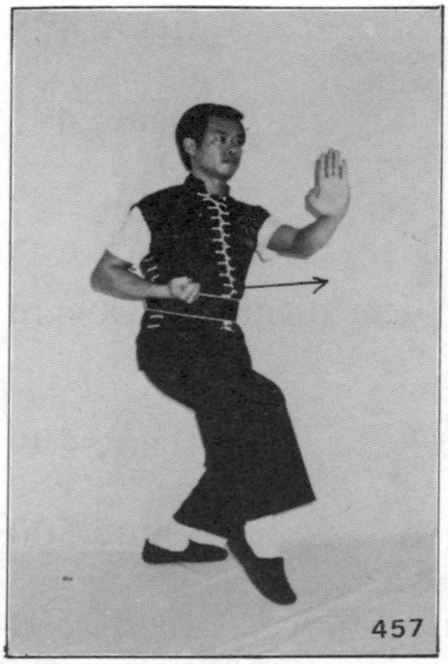
457

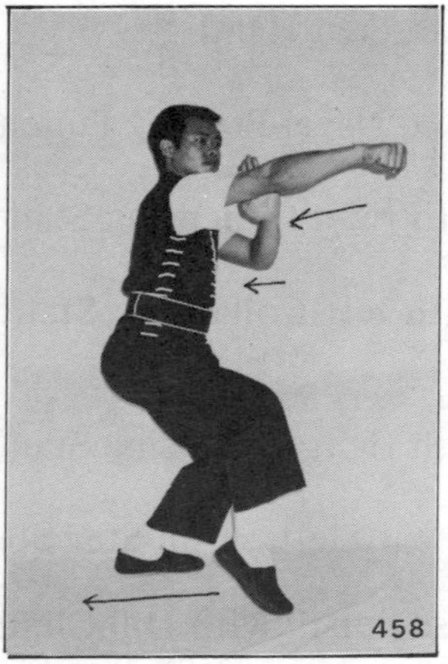
458

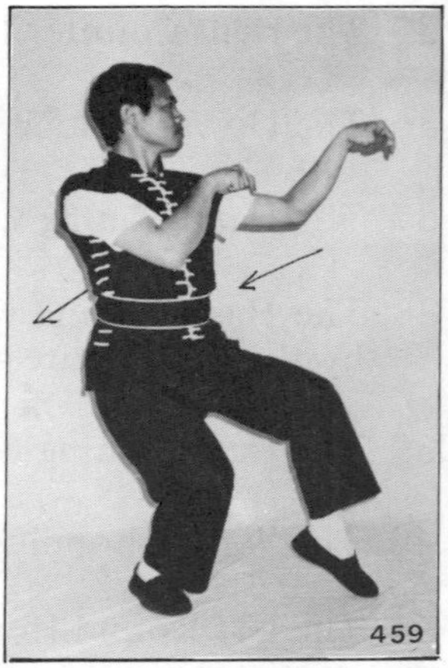
459

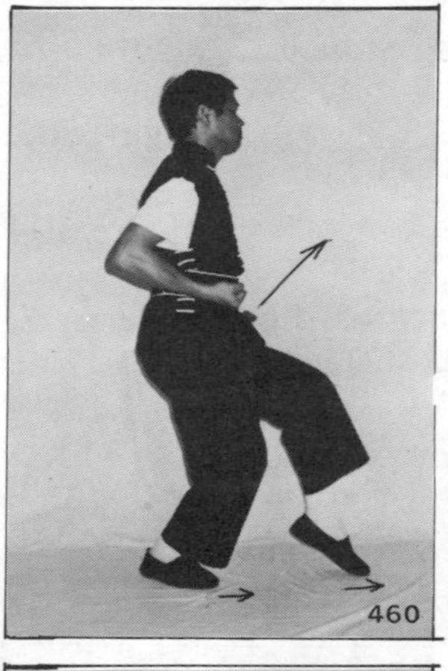
460

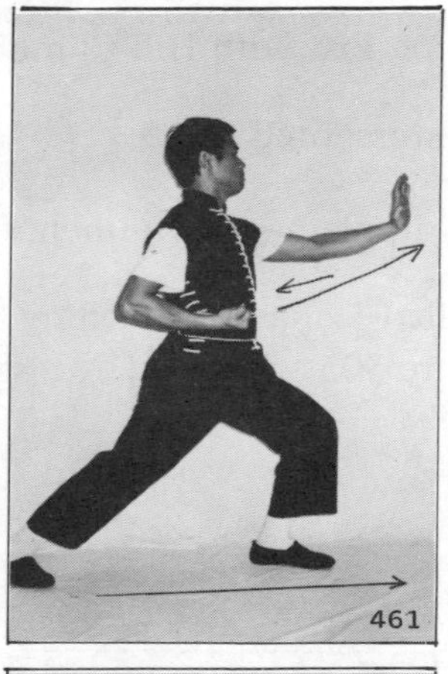
461

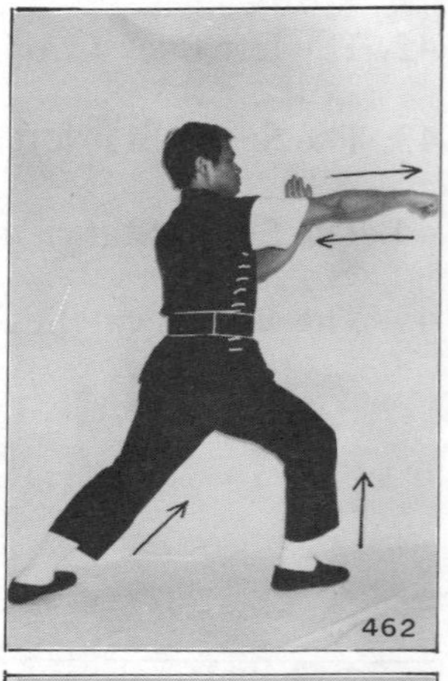
462

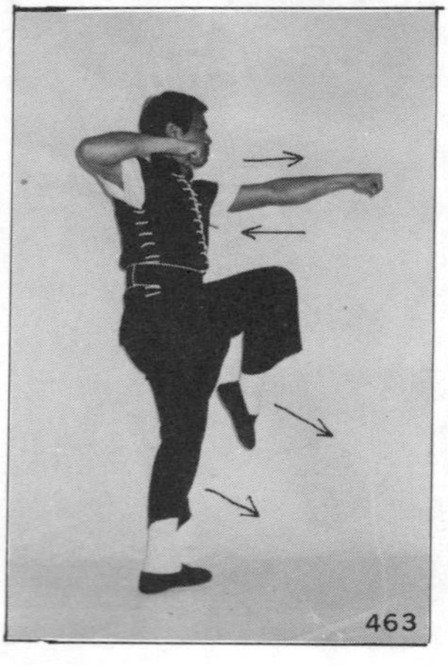
463

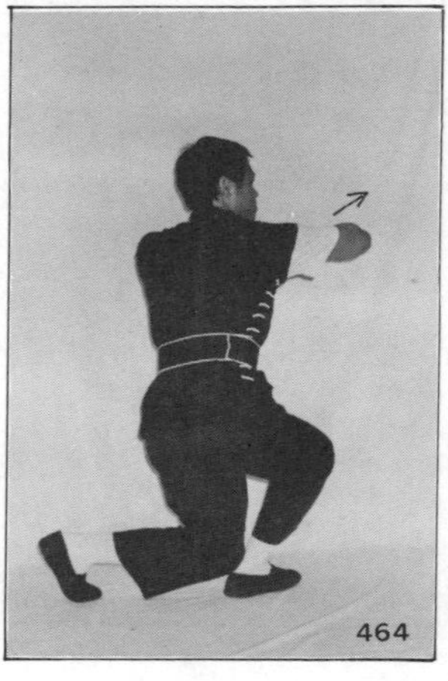
464

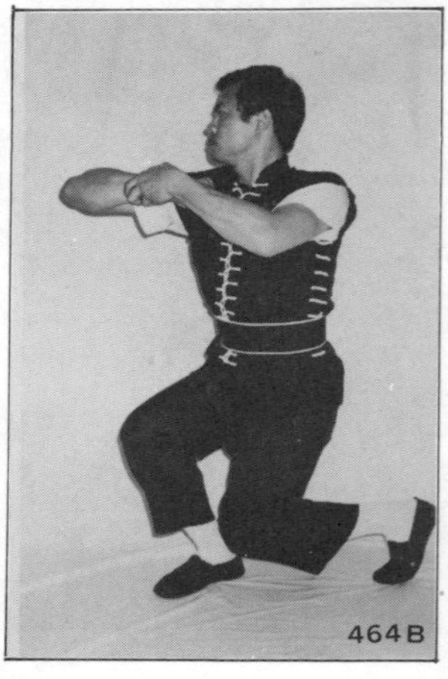
464B

465 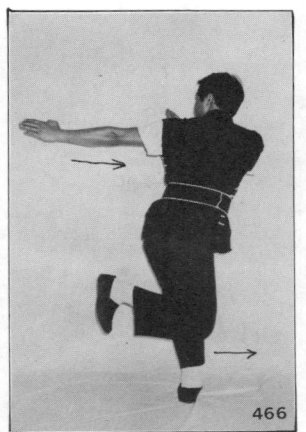 466  467

467B  468  469

470  471  472

107

108

480 481 481B
482 482B 483
483B 484 485

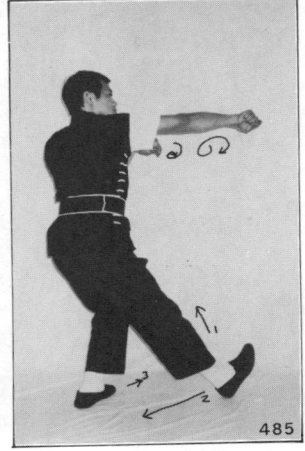

486 487 488
489 490 490B
491 492 493

494

495

496

497

498

499

500

500B

111

501 502 503
504 505 506
507 508

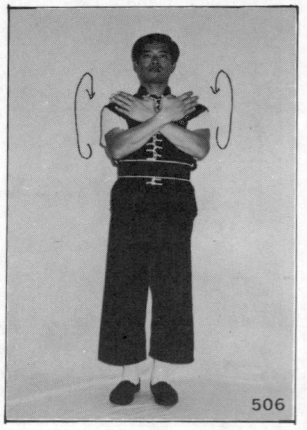

Explanation For Extracted Skills From the Pung Po Boxing Series

THE LITTLE SCOOP WHEEL TIGER—RIDING STANCE 跨虎小翻手

Figure 509—511 shows Master Lee grasps the coming attack at above head with a Tiger-Riding Stance, while he leaves his left grappling hand quickly to force an upward punch at the opponent's Jaw. It is noted that the hanged leg of the Tiger-Riding Stance can kick out at anytime, while the movement of the Horse-Riding can draw close the distance with the opponent.

113

THE MANTIS CATCHING THE CICADA 螳螂捕蟬
Figure 512—514 shows Master Lee circles both of his hands to grasp the opponent's hand from left to right, while the hanged leg is being kick out at anytime.

THE REAR TREASURE—PLUCKING 背後採寶
Figure 515—517 shows the Boxer pushes aside both of his palm at rear coming attack, while he kicks his rear leg backward.

THE HAND—FANING WITH COLLAPSING STANCE 吞踢扇風手

Figure 518—520 Master Lee grasps the coming attack with his right hand, at the same time, he advance his left foot into the rear of the opponent's front leg while he claws horizontally with his left hand, so as to cause the opponent lose his balance.

115

Method of Stretching before Physical Strength Training

It is help to avoid spain or wound caused in excessive movement in physical excercise whenever Joints-loosening activity is sufficiently done before making physical strength training or Kung Fu practising.

PALM—SHAKING 搖手
Figure 312—313 shows the Driller swings at the wrist joint, the aim is to release lively the tendons in the wrist joint.

THE SOOP WHEEL HAND 翻車手
Figure 314—315 shows the Driller circles both of his hands alternatively, so as to loosen his Shoulder joint.

CIRCLING AT KNEE JOINT 提圈腿
Figure 316 shows the Driller lifts up either his legs to circle horizontally left and right, while he cross his fingers to hold at the Knee joint.

316

CIRCLING AT ANKLE JOINT 搖腳踝關節
Figure 317 shows the Driller places the point of his foot resting on ground, so as to circle his heel at the ankle joint from left and right.

317

WAIST—STRETCHING 腰部伸展

Figure 318 shows the Driller circles his body at the waist from left and right.
Figure 319—320 shows the driller bends his waist toward the front and rear.

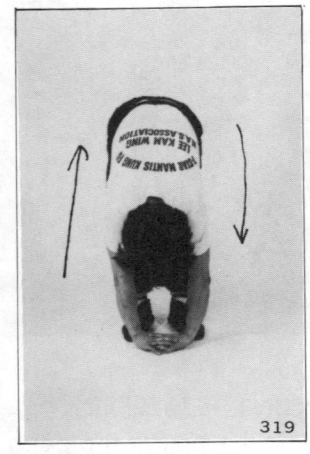

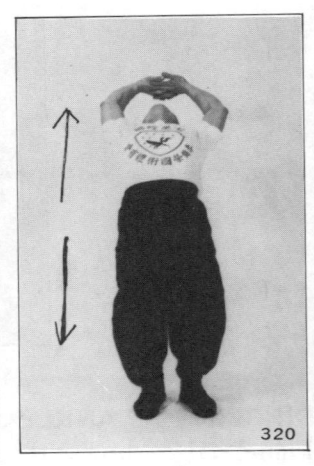

NECK—STRETCHING 頸部伸展

Figure 321—322 shows the Driller swings his head smoothly from left and right.
Figure 323—324 shows the Driller bends his neck forward and backward.
Figure 325 shows the Driller faces upward to circle his forehead from left and right.

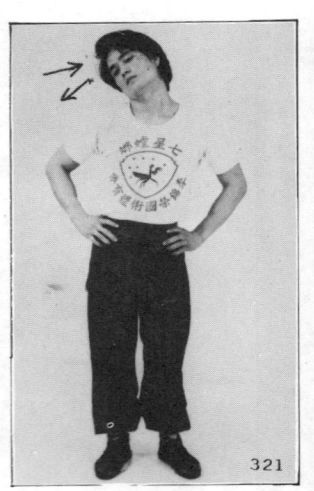

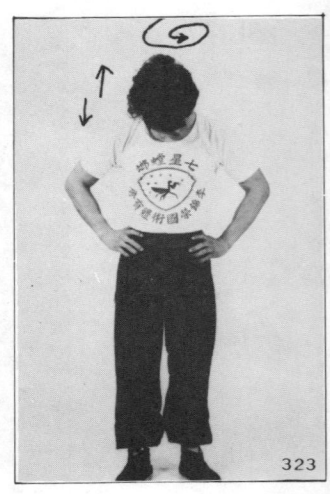

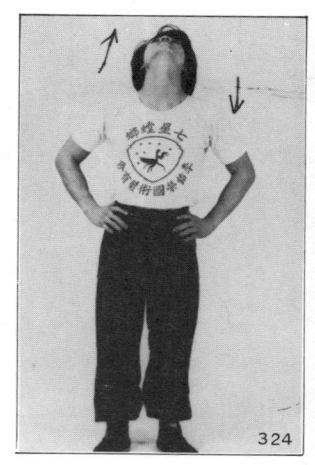

LEG—OVERWHELMING 壓腿

Figure 326 shows the Driller bends his waist to keep the face close to the leg surface. it is worth to note at the begining that the Driller should bend his waist slowly, so as to add pressure and raise the height of the supporting truss day by day.

Figure 327 shows the Driller stretches his left leg backward with the back of his foot facing on ground, while he presses down with his crossed fingers at the kneecape of his right leg so as to lower his body.

Figure 328 shows the Driller stretches aside his left leg with an upturned foot, while he lower his body with the crossed fingers holding at the kneecape of the bent leg.

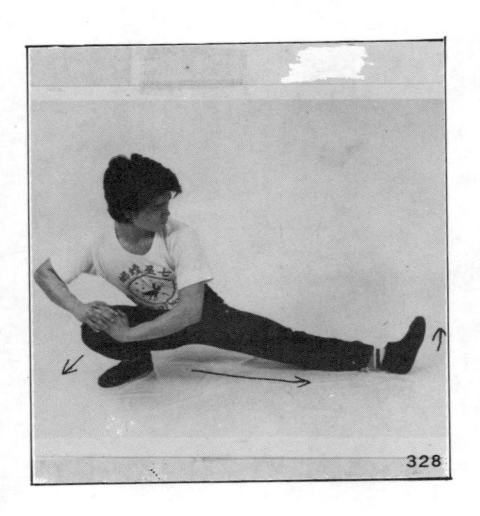

LEG—PILING UP 溜腿
Figure 329-333 shows the Driller Kicks alternatively left and right at the lower portion of the Tibia.

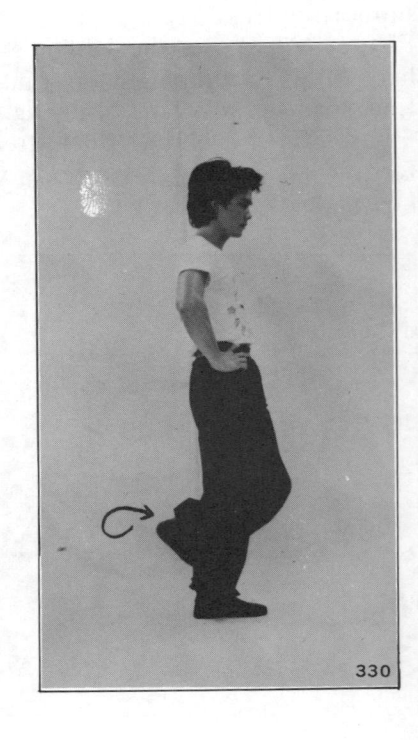

331

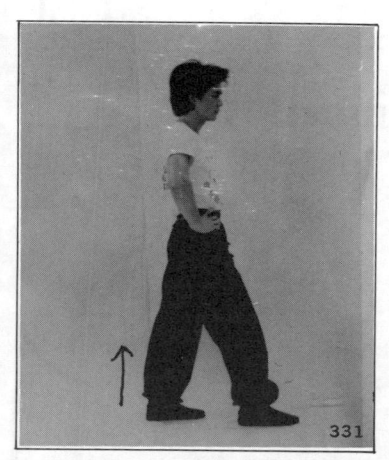

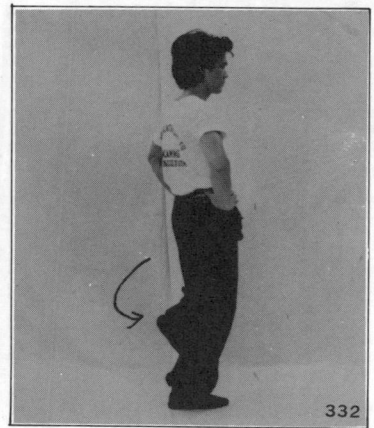

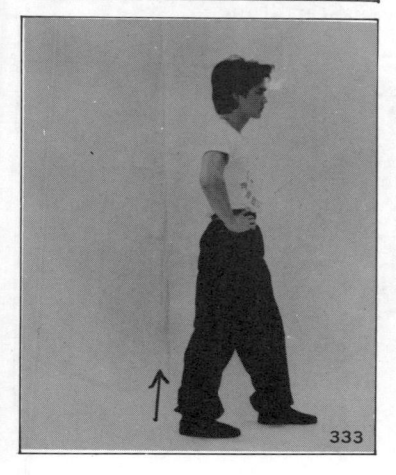

332

333

The Hand - to - Hand Combat

THE INTERCEPTED HAND 刁手
Figure 298–299 shows the Boxer hooks the coming attack with his left hand, while he adds a forced chopping fist at the back of the opponent's neck.

THE SEVEN–STAR DOUBLE INTERCEPTED HAND 七星雙刁手
Figure 300–301 shows the Boxer hooks the coming attack at the opponent's wrist and elbow joint with a Seven Star Stance.

THE SEVEN-STAR COUNTER-GRAPPING HAND 七星纏絲手

Figure 302–303 shows the Boxer holds the opponent's grappling hand downward, while he places a Seven-Star Stance to cause the opponent lose his balance.

THE DOUBLE INTERCEPTED HAND WITH HORSE-RIDING STANCE
馬式雙刁手

Figure 304–305 shows the Boxer hooks the coming attack with his Double Intercepted Hand, while he enters his Horse Riding Stance in to the back of the opponent's leg, so as to cause the opponent loss his balance.

THE INVITATION OF THE WHITE APES 白猿請客
Figure 306-307 shows the Boxer grapples the coming attack at the opponent's wrist and elbow joint with a Monkey Stance.

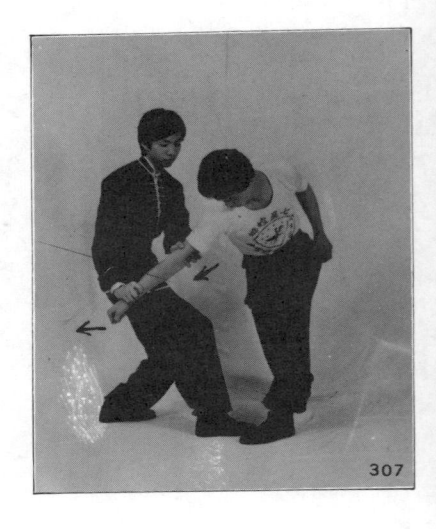

THE FILING PUNCH 措捶
Figure 308-309 shows the Boxer grapples the coming attack, at the same time he pushes his left hand downward at the back of the opponent's palm.

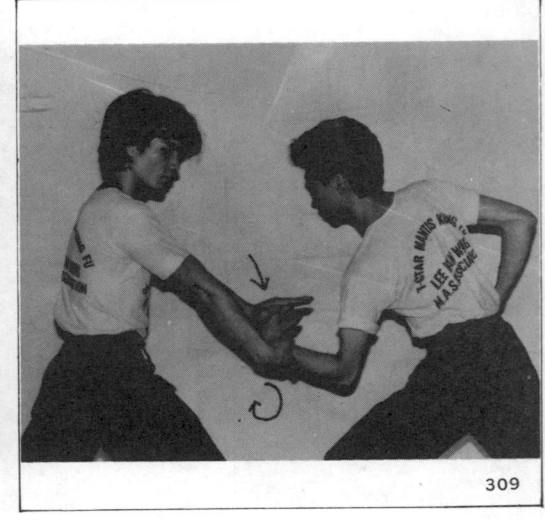

THE HALTING HANDS WITH LEG—PROPPING KICK 封手扑腿

Figure 310—311 shows the Boxer grapples down the coming attack with his double Intercepted Hand, while he props his left leg straightly at the opponent's Kneecape.

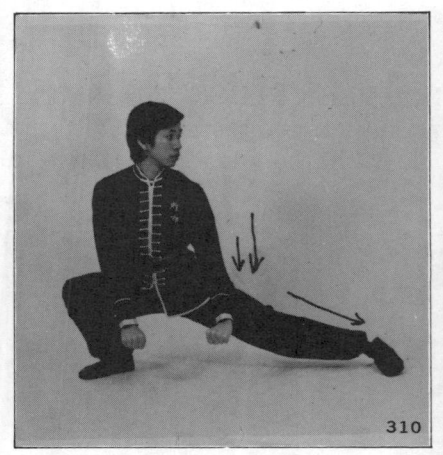

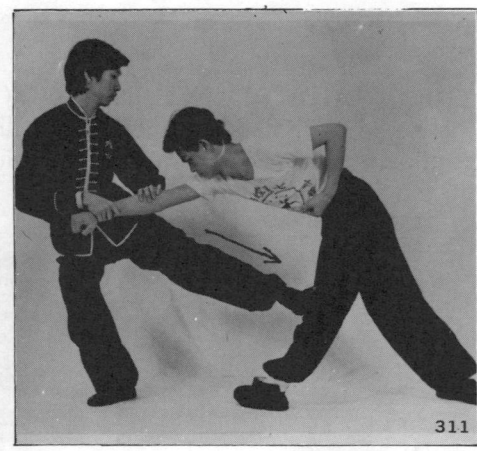

The Twenty - five Fist - fighting Technique

THE STRAIGHT PUNCH IN HOOK GRAPPLE & PLUCK 拘摟採統捶
Figure 239−245 shows the Boxer utilizes his left and right hand with the application of Hook Grapple and pluck, while he adds his left fist to punch ahead.

THE SEVEN-STAR SUPPLEMENTARY PUNCH 七星補捶
Figure 246—247 shows the Boxer places his Seven-Star stance while he push aside his left palm to the right at the same time he forces a straight punch ahead.

THE ROUND HOUSE PUNCH 圈捶
Figure 248—249 shows the Boxer raises his left fist aside from left to right to strike at the opponent's upper part.

127

THE BACK CHOPPING FIST 崩捶
Figure 250-251 shows the Boxer grapples the coming attack with his left hand, while he chops his right fist down at the opponent's face.

THE DRILLING FIST 鑽捶
Figure 252-253 shows the Boxer launches a straight punch from his waist height while he twists his forced fist.

THE NAVEL–PROPPING PUNCH 頂臍捶

Figure 254–255 shows the Boxer raises his left forearm to block the coming attack at above head, at the same time, he launches a horizontal punch at the opponent's navel.

129

THE FILING PUNCH 挫捶
Figure 256–257 shows the Boxer grasps the coming attack with his left hand, while he punches his right fist upward.

256

257

THE BELLY–CAVING PUNCH 窩肚捶
Figure 258–259 shows the Boxer forces a vertical fist at the opponent's belly with a Circle Entering Stance.

258

259

THE GRAPPLING PUNCH 封統捶
Figure 260–262 shows the Boxer forces ahead a left straight punch, while he grasps the coming attack with his right hand.

THE WARD OFF PUNCH 挑統捶
Figure 263–265 show the Boxer forces ahead a left straight forward punch, while he ward off the coming attack with his right arm from left to right.

THE LOWER ROUND HOUSE PUNCH 低圈捶
Figure 266–267 shows the Boxer circles his right forearm downward from right to left at the lower attacking level.

THE WHIPPING FIST 鞭捶
Figure 268–269 shows the Boxer swips aside his right hand to the right with a Horse Riding Stance.

THE CHEST−PIERCING PUNCH 偷心捶
Figure 270−271 shows the Boxer launches a sideway horizontal punch to the right, while grasps the coming attack at abore head.

THE SCOOP WHEEL FIST 翻車捶
Figure 272−273 shows the Boxer circles his stretched left and right forearm downward and upward with a Hill Climbing Stance.

133

THE WHEELING FIST 轆轆捶
Figure 274—275 shows the Boxer circles upward his right forearm from left to right with a Cross-Leg Stance.

THE WHIP—HOOKING FIST 單鞭捶
Figure 276—277 shows the Boxer grasps the coming attack with his left hand, while he pulls his left grappling fist backward. At the same time, he draws back his front leg to hook in his bent right hand with a Tiger Riding Stance.

THE LOWER SWEEPING FIST 低扎捶

Figure 278—279 shows the Boxer holds down his left hand with a Seven-Star Stance, while he forces his stretched right hand to strike at a low level from right to left.

THE DOUBLE BUMPING PUNCH 雙撞捶

Fignre 280—281 shows the Boxer forces both of his powerful fist to bump straightly ahead.

THE CHOPPING FIST 劈捶

Figure 282—283 shows the Boxer raises his right hand to strike down a powerful chopping fist, while he draws back his left hand by the side of his right shoulder.

THE LITTLE SCOOP WHEEL FIST 小翻車捶

Figure 284—285 shows the Boxer raises his right forearm at above head, while he launches his left fist to punch upward.

THE POWER–FORCING FIST 勢捶
Figure 286–287 shows the Boxer holds a powerful fist to force down from right to left.

THE UPWARD BLOCK STRAIGHT PUNCH 掛統捶
Figure 288–290 shows the Boxer launches a straight punch with his right fist, while he raises his left forearm to block the coming attack.

THE CROSS FIST 十字捶

Figure 291–293 shows the Boxer sweeps aside both of his powerful fists from left to right, while he forces his left hand in front and right hand at behind.

291

292

293

THE TIGER–STRIKING FIST 打虎捶

Figure 294–295 shows the Boxer forces down his stretched right hand with the Proping stance while he raises his left forearm upward.

294

295

THE SHOOT UP FIST 冲天炮捶

Figure 296-297 shows the Boxer punches his right fist upward with a Filching Stance while he holds his left hand at the right.

The Wooden Dummy Practising

PART I

The Seven-Star Wooden Dummy is generated from the application of the Seven Method of Long-Striking and Short-Striking in the Seven-Star Mantis Style.

By practising the Seven-Star Wooden Dummy, The learner will get training of strong musels for parts of the body and the active variation of the limbs.

METHOD OF THE THREE-STAR HAND AND UPWARD BLOCK
三星掛手法

1. Figure 596 shows a preceding posture, placing the upturned palms front and rear with a Tiger-Riding Stance.

2. Figure 597 shows Master Lee advances his right leg one step with a Hill-Climbing Stance, while he strike his right forearm by the left at the lower bracket of the dummy.

3. Figure 598 shows Master Lee wards his right forearm upward by the right at the middle bracket of the dummy.

4. Figure 599 shows Master Lee strike his right forearm by the right at the lower bracket of the dummy.

5. Figure 600 shows Master Lee raises his right forearm to block at the upper left bracket of the dummy, while he punch his left fist straightly at the upper part of the dummy, with a Horse-Riding Stance.

6. Figure 601 shows Master Lee draws back his left straight punch to

block at the upper right bracket of the dummy, while he launches his right straight punch at the upper part of the dummy.

7. Figure 602 shows Master Lee changes a right Hill-Climbing Stance to strike his left forearm by the right at the lower bracket of the dummy.

8. Figure 603 shows Master Lee wards his left forearm upward by the left at the middle bracket of the dummy.

9. Figure 604 shows Master Lee strikes his left forearm the left at the lower bracket of the dummy.

10. Figure 605 shows Master Lee raises his left forearm to block at the upper right bracket of the dummy, while he launches a straight punch at the upper part of the dummy with a Horse-Riding Stance.

11. Figure 606 shows Master Lee changes a reverse action to punch at the upper part of the dummy.

12. Figure 607-616 shows the same practising method from action 2 to 11.

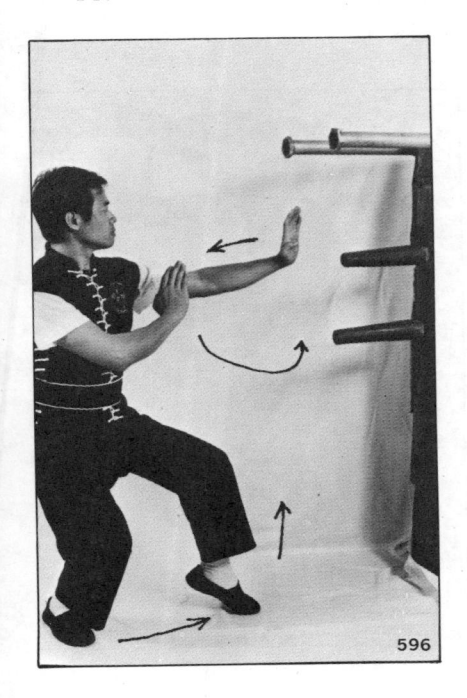

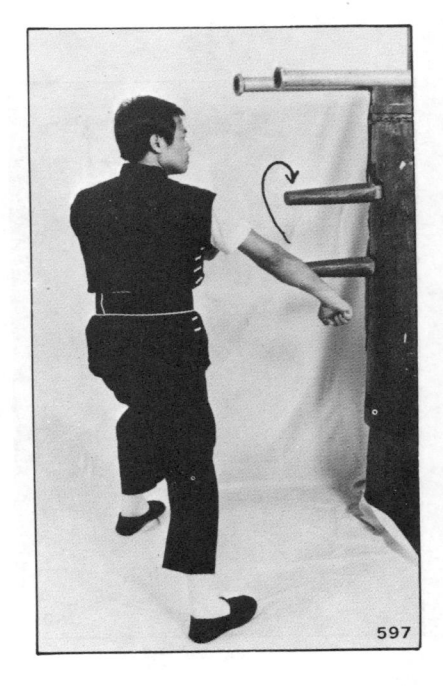

598

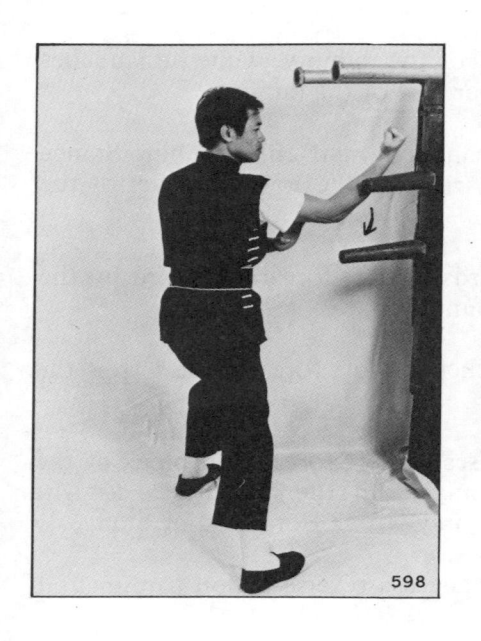

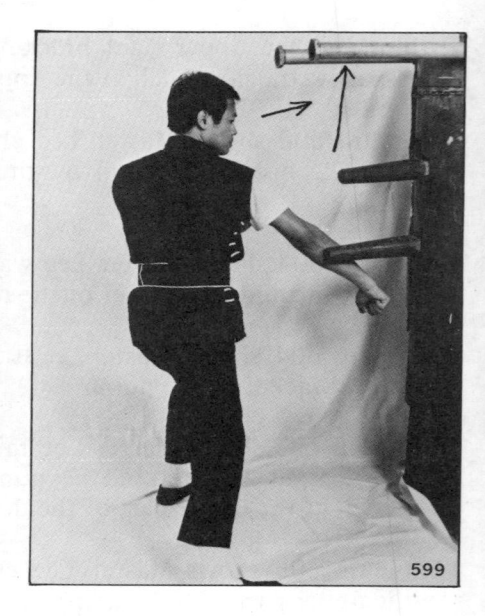

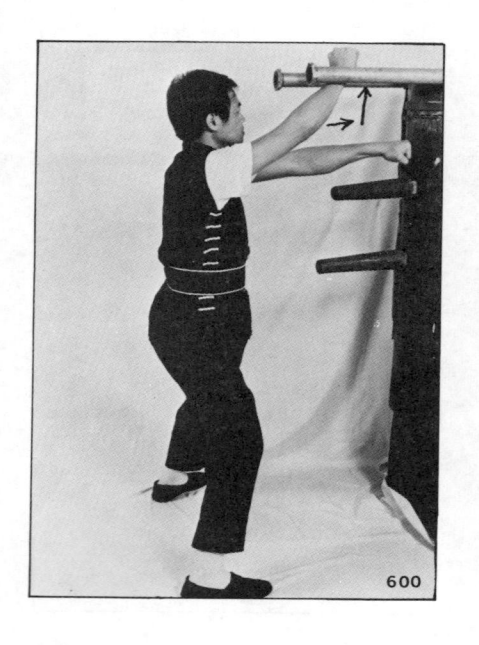

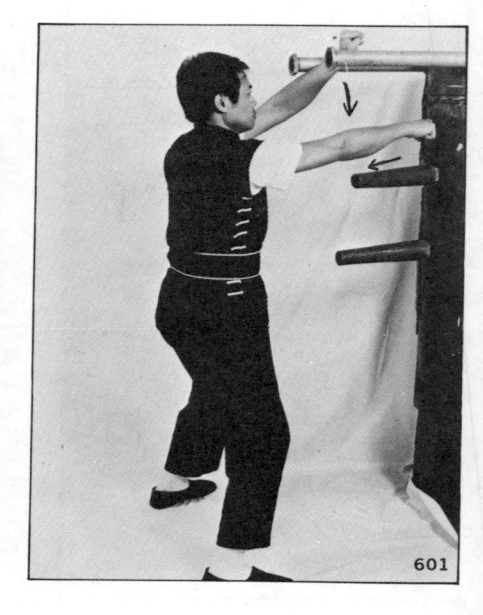

599

600

601

142

143

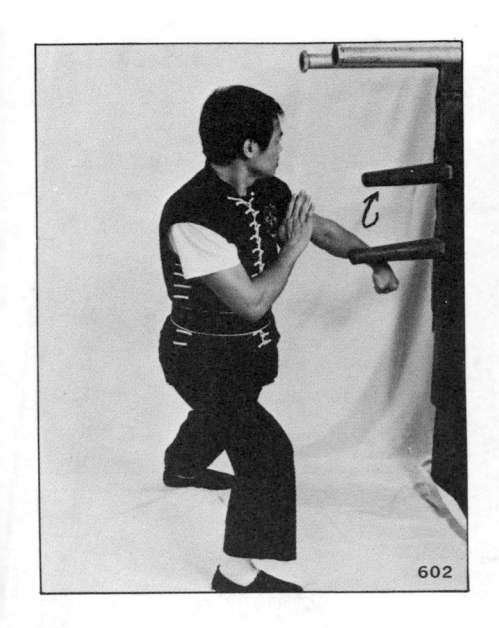

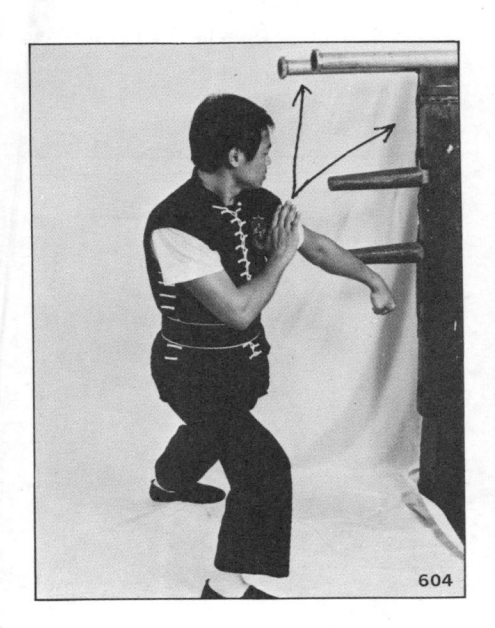

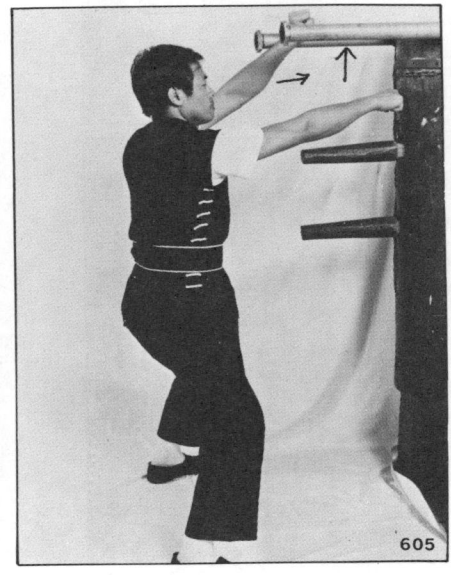

144

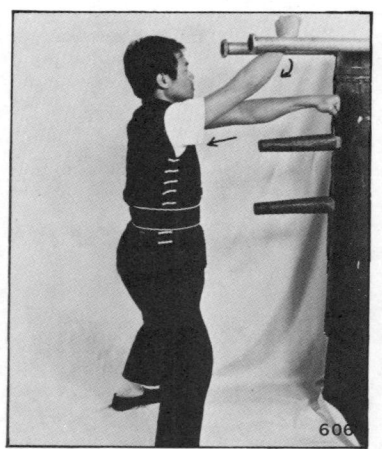

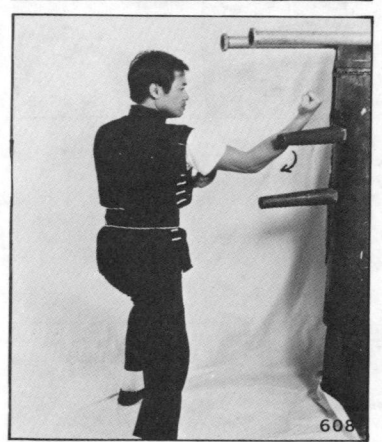

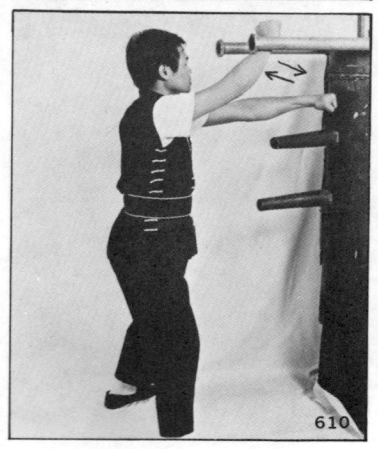

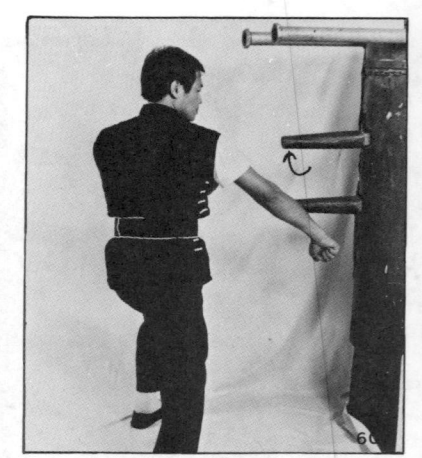

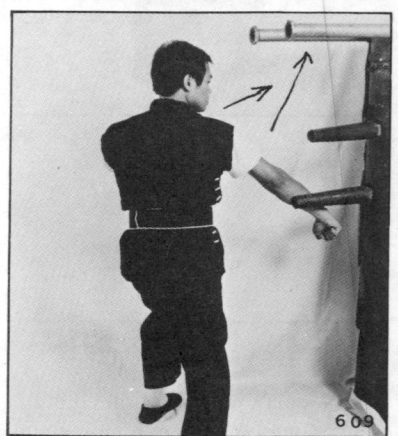

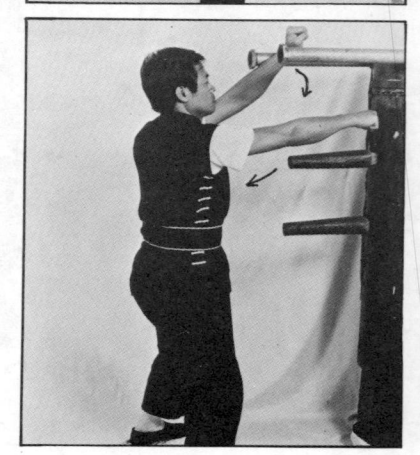

145

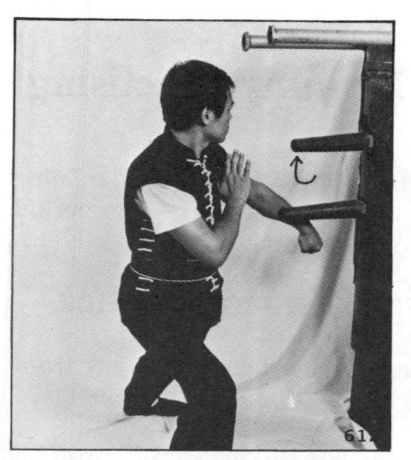

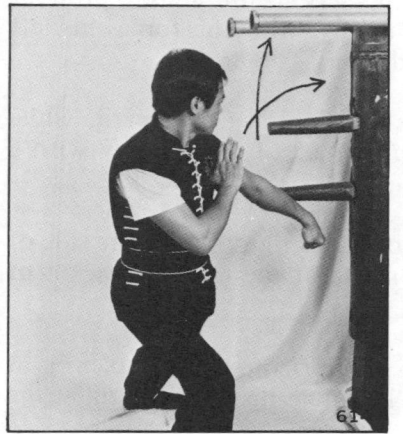

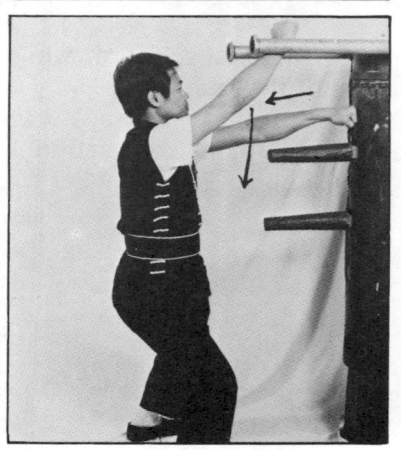

PART II
The Method of Wooden Dummy Practising

The principle of the Wooden Dummy Practising —Part II is a training of the co-operative application for both of hands and legs. The period for practising shall keep five minutes up to one hours.

METHOD OF THE POWER-FORCING FIST AND PROPPING KICK
勢捶扎腿法

1. Figure 617 shows a preceding posture placing the forced fists front and rear with a left Tiger-Riding Stance.

2. Figure 618 shows Master Lee advance his left leg one step to prop his right foot at the lower part of the dummy, while he forces his left forearm at the middle bracket of the dummy.

3. Figure 619 shows Master Lee draws his right leg backward, while he forces a straight punch at the upper part of the dummy with a left Hill Climbing Stance.

4. Figure 620 shows Master Lee draws back his right fist by the side of the waist, while he forces his left forearm at the middle bracket of the dummy.

5. Figure 621 shows Master Lee raises his horizontal foot to prop at the lower part of the dummy, while he forces his left forearm at the middle bracket of the dummy.

6. Figure 622 shows Master Lee draws his right leg backward, while he forces a straight punch at the upper part of the dummy.

7. Figure 623-627 shows a reverse practising method from action 1 to 6 with a preceding posture of right Hill-Climbing Stance.

AND SO ON ....

147

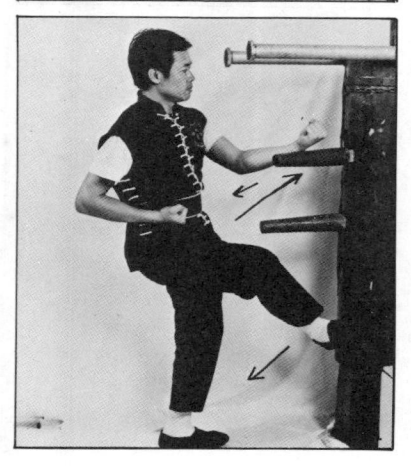

624

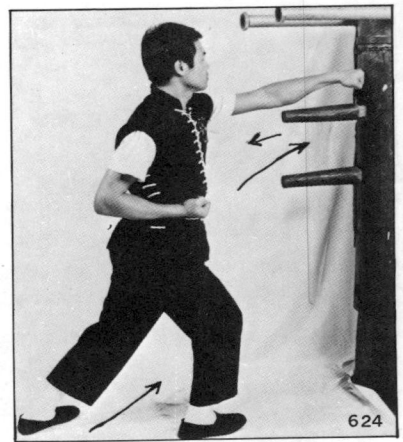

625

627

PART III
The Method of Wooden Dummy Practising

The Wooden Dummy Practising part three is to introduce the application of the Seven keywords in Long-Striking and Short-Striking commonly used in offense and self-defense.

THE SEVEN KEYWORDS IN LONG-STRIKING AND SHORT-STRIKING
1. SHIH   (Power-forcing)   勢
2. CHA   (Prop)   扎
3. FENG   (Halt)   封
4. KWA   (Block)   掛
5. SHAN   (Dodge)   閃
6. PU   (Supplement)   補
7. PENG-TA   (Chop)   崩打

The Application of the Seven Keywords in Long-Striking and Short-Striking

1. **THE SEVEN-STAR POSTURE** 七星勢
   Figure 629 shows a preceding posture of the Seven-Star Mantis Style commonly used in offense and self-defense.

2. **THE POWER-FORCING WITH HILL-CLIMBING STANCE** 登山步勢捶
   Figure 630 shows Master Lee advances his left leg one step with a Hill-Climbing Stance, while he forces his left forearm at the middle bracket of the dummy.

3. **THE PROPPING KICK** 扎腿
   Figure 631 shows Master Lee props his right horizontal foot at the lower part of the dummy, the use the propping kick is to strike at the knee joint of the opponent.

4. **THE HALTING PALM** 封掌
   Figure 632 shows Master Lee turns down his left fist to grasp at the

149

middle bracket of the dummy, while he forces an upturned right thrusting palm at the upper head of the dummy.

5. **THE RIGHT UPWARD BLOCK AND STRIAGHT PUNCH** 右掛統捶
   Figure 633 shows Master Lee raises his right forearm to block at the upper left backet of the dummy, while he forecs a left straight punch at the upper part of the dummy.

6. **THE LEFT UPWARD BLOCK AND STRAIGHT PUNCH** 左掛統捶
   Figure 634 shows Master Lee raise his left forearm to block at the upper right bracket of the dummy, while he forces a right straight punch at the upper part of the dummy with a Horse-Riding Stance.

7. **THE DOOR-SHUTTERING KICK IN DODGE** 閃步撩陰腳
   Figure 635 shows Master Lee grasps the middle bracket of the dummy with his right hand, while he raises a Door-Shuttering Kick at the lower part of the dummy.

8. **THE SUPPLEMENTARY FIST** 補捶
   Figure 636 shows Master Lee pushes aside with his left upturned palm at the middle bracket of the dummy, while he forces his left fist to punch at the middle part of the dummy.

9. **THE CHOPPING FIST** 崩捶
   Figure 637 shows Master Lee turns his left palm to grasp the middle bracket of the dummy, while he raises his left fist upward to punch at the upper head of the dummy.

10. **THE LEFT WARD OFF FIST AND BUMPING KICK** 左挑手撐腿
    Figure 638 shows Master Lee moves his right leg one step by the right. At the same time he bumps his left foot at the lower part of the dummy, while he raises his left forearm to ward at the upper left bracket of the dummy.

11. **THE RIGHT WARD OFF FIST AND BUMPING KICK** 右挑手撐腿
    Figure 639 shows Master Lee places his left leg down by the left, at the same time, he bumps his right leg at the lower part of the dummy, while he raise his right forearm to ward at the upper right bracket of the dummy.

12. **THE HALTING PALM** 封掌
    Figure 640 shows Master Lee places down his right leg to grasp the middle bracket of the dummy with his left hand, while he force an

upturned right thrusting palm at the upper head of the dummy.

AND SO ON . . . . . .

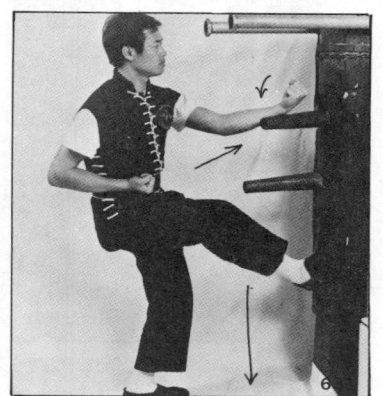

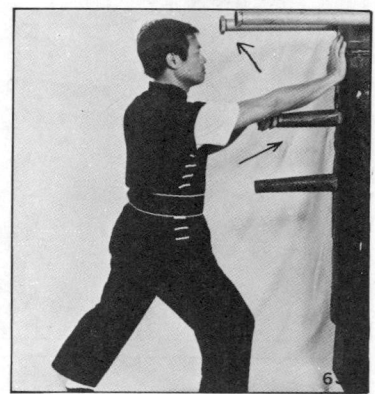

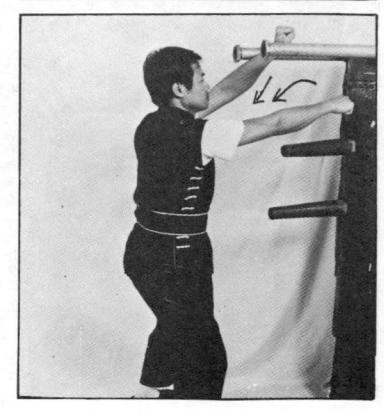

152

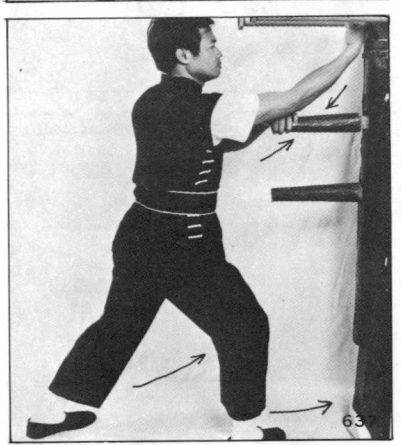

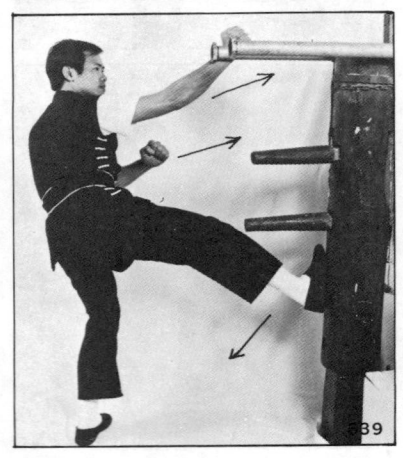

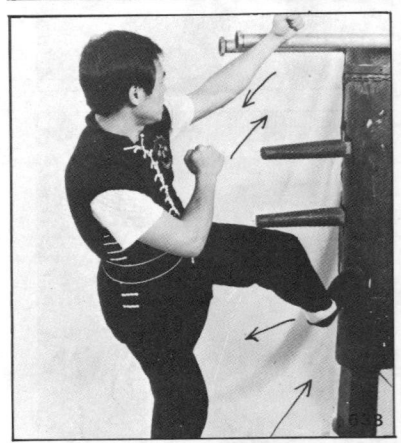

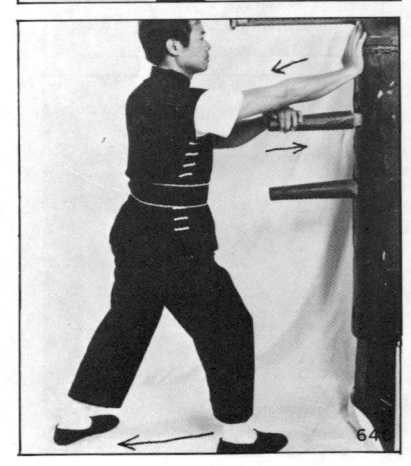

Method of Physical Strength Training

1. **DUMBELL IN STRAIGHT PUNCH PRACTICE** 啞鈴直拳練習
   Figure 335-337 shows the Driller pushes ahead a straight punch left and right by holding a dumbell in hand, the weight of the dumbell can be added little by little following a period of practising.

2. **ROLLING IN RIGID HAND** 碌橋手
   Figure 338—339 shows the Driller bends his elbows to roll the steel pipe inward, and stretches his forearms to roll the steel pipe outward. the weight of the steel pipe can be added little by lettle following a period of practising.

153

338

339

3. **FINGERS—GRIPING** 指抓法

Figure 340-341 shows the Driller uses both of the last three fingers of his hands to roll up the dumbell with the act of strength from the wrist.

340

341

4. **INTERCEPT HAND PRACTISING IN PAIR** 刁手對練

Figure 342-347 shows the Drillers grasp each other in a counter-intercept hand, while they push it toward the left and pull it backward to the right in turn.

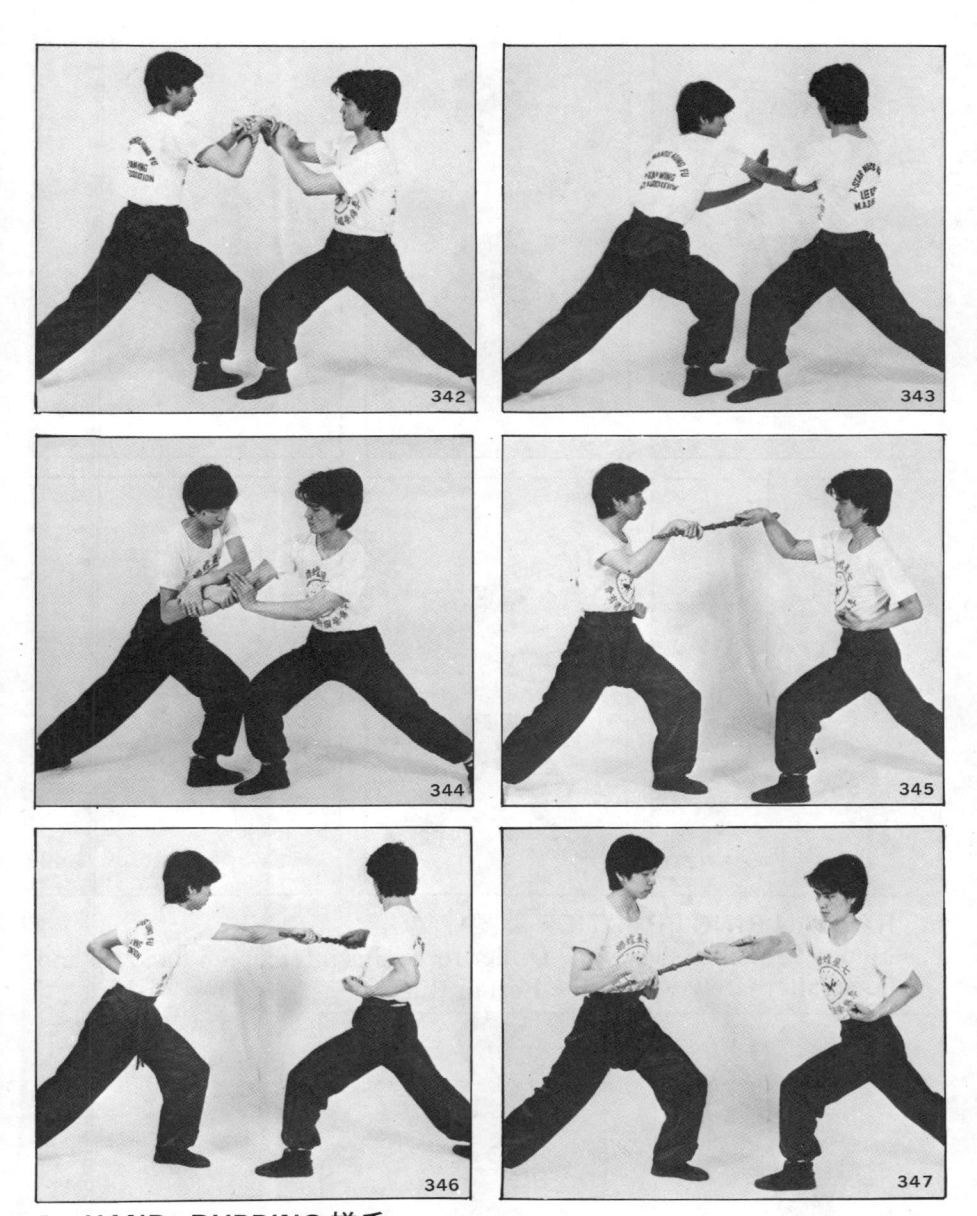

5. HAND—RUBBING 搓手

Figure 349—354 shows the Driller rubs both of his forearm against each other alternately, the aim of the Hand-Rubbing is to enable musels of the forearm to suffer from greater pain and become elastic.

155

6. RATTAN RING PRACTICE 藤圈練習法

Figure 355–356 shows the Driller forces his intercepted hand up and down alternately within the Rattan Ring.

156

7. TENSION STRENGTH PRACTICE 拉力練習

Figure 357 shows the Driller pulls ahead a group of tensioned springs alternately left and right.

8. THE THREE—STAR HAND AND LEG—SPROUTING PRACTISING IN PAIR 三星手揪腿二人對練

1) Figure 358 the Drillers posture a Horse—Riding Stance against each other.
2) Figure 359 the Drillers strike their right forearm slopping down by the left.
3) Figure 360, the Drillers push their right forearm upward to resist by the right.
4) Figure 361 the Drillers strike their right forearm downward by the right.
5) Figure 362 the Drillers grasp each other with a Horse—Riding Stance.
6) Figure 363 the Drillers raise their right leg upward by the left.
7) Figure 364 Drillers kick their right leg backward to the right.
8) Figure 365 Drillers grasp their right forearm each other with Horse—Riding Stance.
9) Figure 366 Drillers Change to strike their left forearm slopping down by the right.

10) Figure 367 Drillers push their left forearm upward to resist by the left.
11) Figure 368 Drillers strike their left forearm slopping down by the left.
12) Figure 369 Drillers grasp their left forearm each other with a Hill—Climbing Stance.
13) Figure 370 Drillers raise their left leg upward by the right
14) Figure 371 Drillers kick their left leg backward by the left.
15) Figure 372 Drillers grasp their left forearm each other with Horse—Riding Stance.
16) Figure 373 Drillers strike again their right forearm slopping down by the left and keep on practising the same from action 3—16.

AND SO ON.............

362

363

364

365

366

367

159

368

369

370

371

372

373

The Essence of the Seven - Star Mantis Style

The important points of the Seven-Star Mantis Style is the corporation of both internal training and external training. The internal training based on the spirital energy and the respiratory force. The external training based on the hands, the eyes, the body and the stance-pacing.

1. **The Spirital Energy**
   The Spirital Energy in the Seven-Star Mantis Style is meant to concentrate one's mind in full attention, without having mixed thoughts.

2. **The Respiratory Force**
   The Respiratory Force in the Seven-Star Mantis Style is to mean that force is concentrated, as respiratory energy is not floated.

3. **The Hands**
   The points of the hands application is the fastest of fist-punching is useful, as if the slowest of the fist-punching is helpless.

4. **The Eyes**
   Sharpness of eye sight, which makes acute hands as the eyes catched, while the vague of eye sight makes loss of attention.

5. **The Body**
   The body is active in turning as if the tardy of the body can cause irregularily movement.

6. **The Stance-pacing**
   The accuracy of the Stance-pacing can give quick attack when a fissured opportunity is being found, in different action on change of situation, and inacuracy of Stance-pacing can cause one lose his control in offense and defense.

The Principle Method Of Offense In The Seven-Star Mantis Style

1. Taking care of up and down
   to get the lower part while striking upward, to get the upper part while striking downward.
2. Dodging left and right
   to defense the right while attacking the left, to defense the left while attacking the right.
3. Going ahead bravely while watching the three ways at the upper, middle and lower direction
   to resist coming attack while attacking the opponent, to attack the opponent while in resisting, to go ahead while dissolving the coming attact.
4. Nothing need for defense is merely just to attack without resisting.
5. Rigid Leg can moves lively on ground.
6. Attacking quickly with Mantis Stance-Pacing.
7. Eyes watched while hands reached, concentration of spirital energy in mind.
8. Turning of body as following steps.
9. Going ahead and setting back in due cause.
10. To achieve a united movement of the spirital energy and respiratory force. The hands, the eyes, the body and the Stance-pacing.

The Striking Method of Keeping Apart in Leg-kicking
In figures 579–580 shows Master Lee launches a door-shuttering Kick, while his upper body is keeping apart from the opponent.

The Method of Attacking while Resisting
In figures 581–582 shows Master Lee utilizes the supplementary punch with Hill-climbing Stance to puch aside the attacking forward punch while he props his left palm straightly at the upper part of the opponent.

The Method of Hand-neglecting
In figures 583–584 shows Master Lee dodges by the left to escape an attacking straight punch, while he keeps a distance to kick at the opponent's lateral surface of waist with the Door-shuttering Kick from a Tiger-Riding Stance.

The Method of Mantis Pacing
The driller's eyes watches ahead at the front part of their palms and bends slightly their foreleg. As they posture a right arm in front, they circle around a target by the left. As they posture a left arm in front, they circle around a target by the reverse direction. (585A - 585E)

579

580

581

582

583

584

163

585A

585B

585C

585D

585E

The Analysis of Forces in the Seven - Star Mantis Style 拳之勁力分析

THE LONG FORCE 長勁
Most punches of the Seven-Star Mantis Style are derived from posting fist at waist side as a purpose to corperate forces from waist and shoulder which is named the positive force.

THE SHORT FORCE 短勁
The delivery of the reserved force from waist, shoulder, elbow and wrist by corperation of wrist-turning is named the negative force.

THE BORROWED FORCE 借力打法
(Method of Dispeling Thousand Weight by a Quater)

The theory of the Borrowed Force is explained to give reason why a balance, or a pound which can uplift a more bigger volume than itself.

For example I — The Seven Star Suplementary punch, which can dissolve a forced straight punch by pushing a left hand to dispel at the wrist of the comming attack as shown in figure J1 — J3.

For example 2 — The Peach-offering of the Mantis. As a straight punch striked from the opponent. One of the Borrowed Force shown in figure J4 — J6, is to dissolve a straight punch by pushing upward with the right palm at the elbow joint and the left palm at the wrist of the opponent, while a Door-Shutting Kick is applied.

166

For example 3 — The Leg-Sprouting Method, shown in figure J7 — J8, The Boxer uses his right Intercepted Hand to shutter the straight forward punch from the opponent. As soon as he uses his left intercept hand to hood backward at the neck of the opponent he kicks upward at the back of the opponents front leg to cause the opponent lose his balance.

The Intermediate Level of the Seven - Star Mantis Style practising series - The BLACK — TIGER — CROSS

1. The Seven-Star Mantis Catching the Cicada. fig.529-530
   七星螳螂捕蟬
2. The Seven-Star Counter-Intercept Hand. fig.531
   七星纏絲手
3. The Seven-Star Upward Block Straight Punch. fig.532
   七星左掛統
4. The Hand-Claping with right Chest-piercing Kick. fig.533
   拍手穿心腿
5. The Seven-Star right Supplementary Fist. fig.534
   七星右補捶
6. The Lower Circling Fist with Leg-Bouncing Stance. fig.535
   蹤步低圈捶
7. The left Propping palm with Tiger-Riding Stance. fig.536
   跨虎左頂掌
8. The right Elbow-Striking with Circle-Entering Stance. fig.537
   X環右叠肘
9. The right Back Chopping Fist with Attention Stance. fig.538
   中平右崩捶
10. The Door-Shuttering Hand with Collapsing Stance (The Lower Mantis catch the cicada) 吞蹋撩陰手／螳螂低捕蟬 fig.539
11. The right Back Chopping Fist with Attention Stance. fig.540
    中平右崩捶
12. The Lower Mantis catching the Cicada fig.541
    螳螂低捕蟬
13. The right Back Chopping Fist with Attention Stance fig.542
    跨虎左挑統捶
14. The Lower Mantis catching the cicada fig.543
    螳螂低捕蟬
15. The left ward off punch with Tiger-Riding Stance fig.542
    跨虎左挑統捶

16. The Seven-Star Ward off chopping Fist　　　　　fig.543-544
　　七星挑劈捶
17. The Millstone Palm with Hill-Climbing Stance　　fig.545
　　登山磨盆掌
18. The right Back Chopping Fist with Chest-Piercing Kick　fig.546-547
　　右崩捶穿心腿
19. The left Filing Palm with Hill-climbing Stance　　fig.548
　　登山左措掌
20. The right Filing Palm with Hill-climbing Stance　fig.549
　　登山右措掌
21. The Shoot-up Punch with Hill-Climbing Stance　　fig.550
　　登山冲天炮捶
22. The Cross Fist　　　　　　　　　　　　　　　　fig.551
　　十字捶
23. The right Round House Punch with Hill-Climbing Stance　fig.552
　　登山右圈捶
24. The Seven-Star left Mantis Catching the cicada　　fig.553
　　七星左螳螂捕蟬
25. The Seven-Star left Eyes-plucking　　　　　　　fig.554
　　七星左探眼
26. The Seven-Star Mantis Spies cave　　　　　　　fig.555
　　七星螳螂探洞
27. The Seven-Star right Mantis catches the cicada　　fig.556
　　七星右螳螂捕蟬
28. The Seven-Star left Eyes-plucking　　　　　　　fig.557
　　七星左探眼
29. The Seven-Star Mantis Spying cave　　　　　　　fig.558
　　七星螳螂探洞
30. The Seven-Star Mantis Counter-Intercept Hand　　fig.559
　　七星纏絲手
31. The upward Block with left Eyes-Plucking　　　　fig.560
　　掛統左探眼
32. The Seven-Star right Supplementary punch with Hand-skiming
　　脫手補捶　　　　　　　　　　　　　　　　　　fig.561-562
33. The Mantis catching the cicada　　　　　　　　fig.563-565
　　螳螂捕蟬

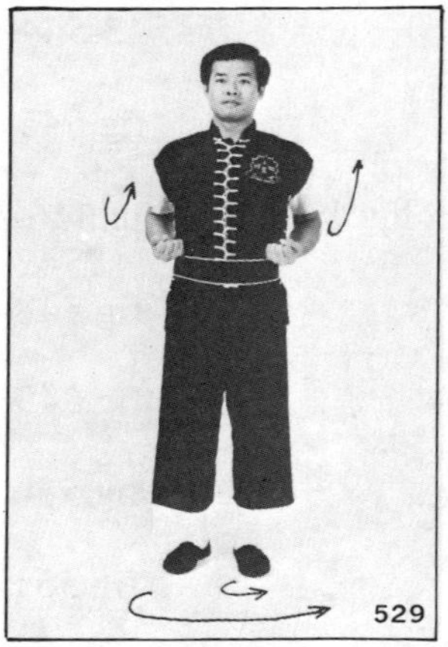
529

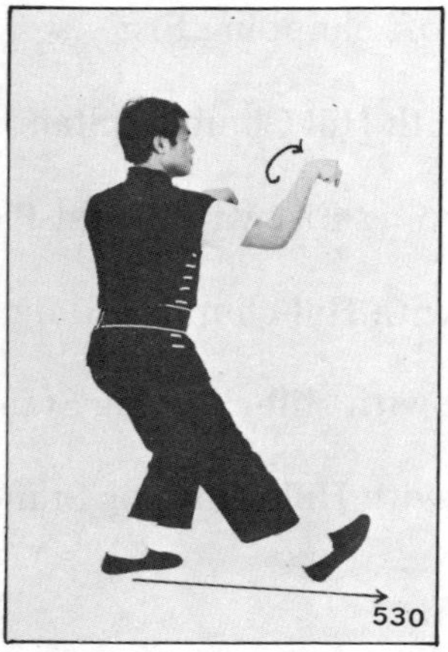
530

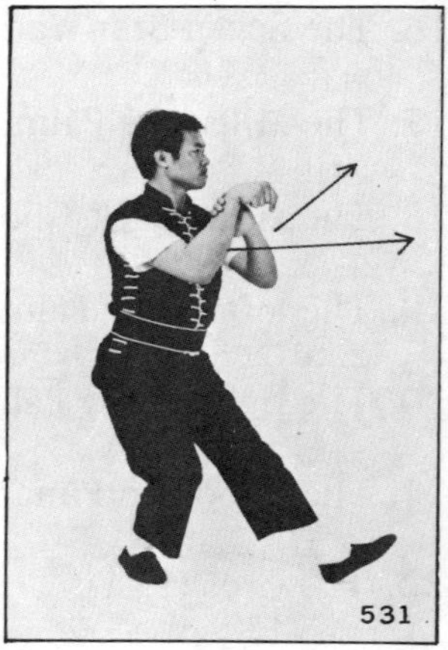
531

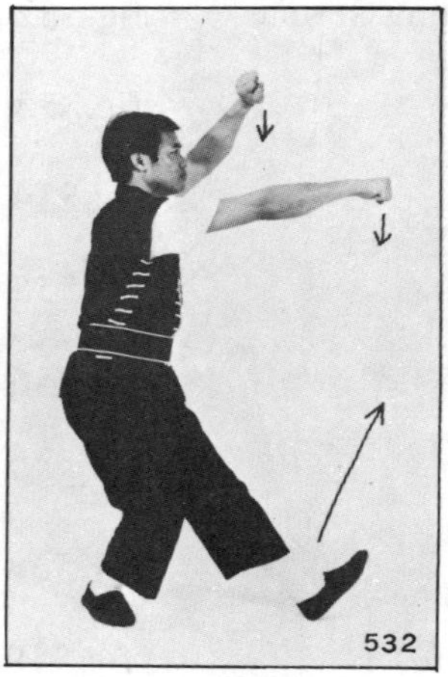
532

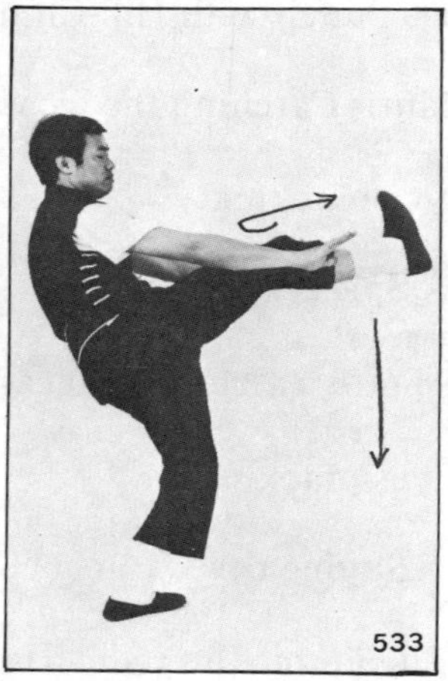
533

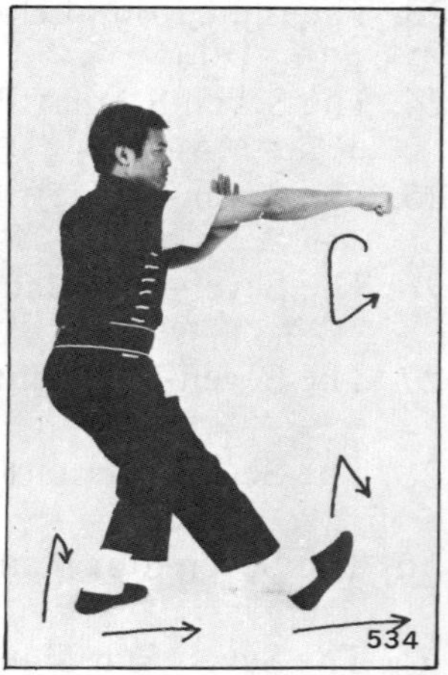
534

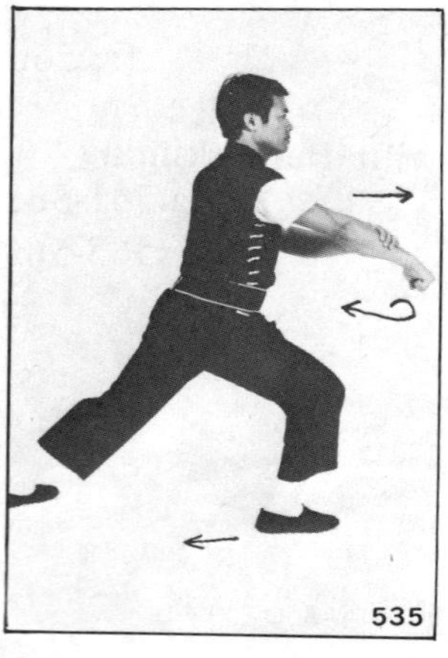
535

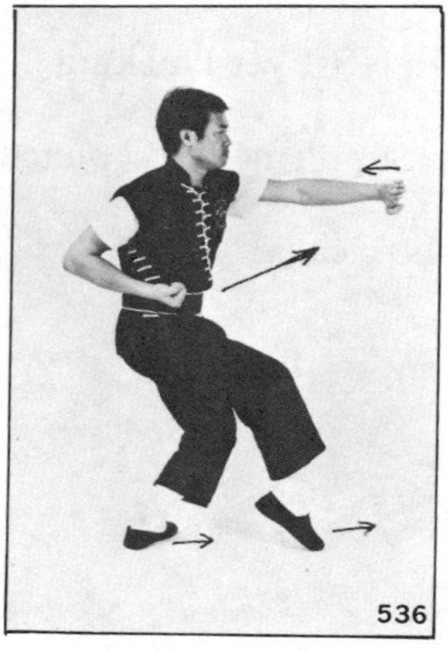
536

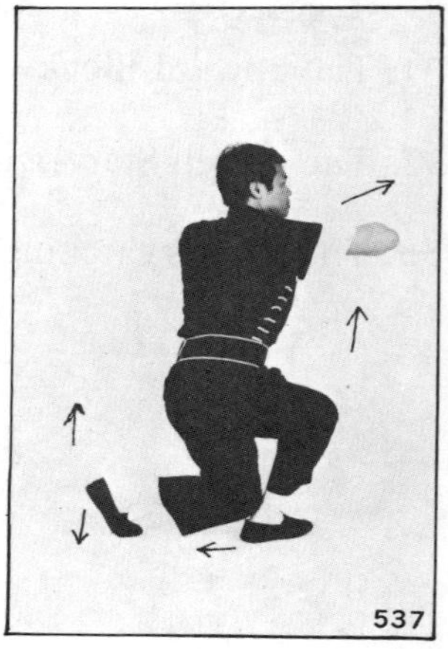
537

171

547
548
549
550
551
552
553
554
555

172

556
557
558
559
560
561
562
563
564

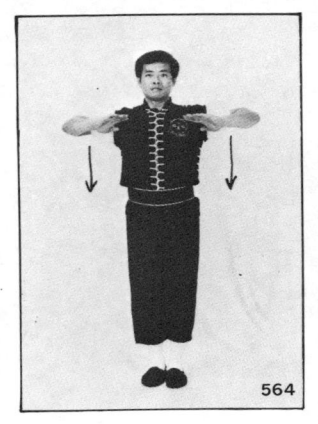

173

565

Explanation For Extracted From The BLACK TIGER CROSS

THE SEVEN—STAR MANTIS CATCHING THE CICADA 七星螳螂捕蟬
Figure 566—568 shows Master Lee grasps the coming attack with his double intercept hand from right to the left, at the same time, he bumps his right foot at the shinbone of the opponent's front leg.

175

THE SEVEN—STAR COUNTER—GRAPPLING HAND 七星纏絲手

Figure 569—571 shows Master Lee turns his right fist to make a Counter-Grappling hand at opponent's right arm, while he presses down the opponent's attacking Hand to prop down the opponent's front leg.

THE HAND—CLAPING WITH CHEST-PIERCING KiCK 拍手穿心腿

Figure 572—574 shows Master Lee halts down the opponent's Double Straight Punch, while he bumps up his right leg at the opponent's front chest.

THE LEFT—FILING PALM 左措掌

Figure 575—578 shows Master Lee raises his right hand to grasp the opponent's coming attack upward, while he pushes his left horizontal palm upward at the opponent's elbow joint.

177

178

The Advance Level of The Seven - Star Mantis Style practising Series — The Mantis out of its cave

1. The Mantis Double Intercepted Hand   fig.641 –641E
   螳螂雙臂勾
2. The Single Claw with Circle Entering Stance   Fig. 642
   入環單臂爪
3. The Filing Punch with right Leg-hanging Stance   fig. 643
   右提腿挫捶
4. The Double Hand-pushing with Toppling Stance   fig. 644–644B
   蹬撲
5. The left Straight Forward Punch with Hill-Climbing Stance   fig. 645
   登山左統捶
6. The right Drilling Punch with Horse-Ring Stance   fig. 646
   馬式右鑽捶
7. The right Filing Punch with Hill-Climbing Stance   fig. 647
   登山右挫捶
8. The Waist-Chopping with left Circle-Entering Stance   fig. 648
   左入環斬腰（左上步）
9. The Straight Punch in Hook Grapple and Pluck   fig. 649
   拘摟採統捶（右後轉）
10. The Waist-Chopping with Circle Entering Stance   fig. 650
    入環斬腰（左上步）
11. The Seven Star Leg-Sprouting Kick   fig. 651 –651B
    七星揪腿
12. The Toppling hand with Filching Stance   fig. 652
    偷步蹬撲
13. The right Round House Punch   fig. 653
    右圈捶
14. The right Hook Grapple and Pluck   fig. 654
    右拘摟採手
15. The Lower Proping Kick   fig. 655
    低軋腿

16. The Lower Mantis catching the cicada　　　fig. 656A – 656C
    螳螂低捕蟬
17. The Seven-Star Lower Proping　　　　　　fig. 657
    七星低軋捶
18. The right counter-Intercept Hand with Leg-Hanging Stance　fig. 658
    提腿右纏絲
19. The Whip-Rolling Hand with Circle Entering Stance　fig. 659
    入環滾捞手
20. The Upward Block-Straight Punch with withdraw Stance　fig. 660
    撤步掛統捶
21. The right Chopping Fist with Hill-Climbing Stance　　fig.661
    登山右劈捶
22. The Eyes-thrusting in Hook Grapple and Pluck (I)　fig. 662 –662A
    拘摟採插眼（一）
23. The Eyes-thursting in Hook Grapple and Pluck (II)　fig. 663 –663A
    拘摟採插眼（二）
24. The left Straight Punch with Tiger-Riding Stance　　fig. 664
    跨虎左統捶
25. The right Drilling Fist with Horse-Riding Stance　　fig. 665
    馬式右鑽捶
26. The Back Chopping Fist　　　　　　　　　fig. 666
    崩捶
27. The Door-Shuttering Kick　　　　　　　　fig. 667
    閉門腿
28. The ward off Palm with Tiger-Riding Stance　　　fig. 668
    跨虎挑掌
29. The right Single Whip-Hooking Fist with Hill-Climbing　fig. 669
    Stance 登山右單鞭
30. The Overwhelming Palm　　　　　　fig. 670A – 670B
    翻天印掌
31. The left ward off straight Punch　　　　　　fig. 671
    左挑統捶
32. The right Drilling Fist with Horse-Riding Stance　　fig.672
    馬式右鑽捶
33. The right Filing Fist with Hill-Climbing Stance　　fig. 673
    登山右挫捶
34. The Waist-Chopping with Circle Entering Stance　　fig. 674
    入環斬腰（左上步）
35. The right Hook Grapple and Pluch with　　fig. 675A – 675C
    Single-Soaring Kick 右拘摟採單飛腿（右轉）
36. The Belly-caving Punch with Circle Entering Stanee　fig. 676
    入環窩肚捶
37. The Back Chopping Fist with Circle Entering Stance 入環崩捶 fig. 677

180

38. The Door-Shuttering Kick   fig. 678
閉門腿（撩陰腿）
39. The Ward off Palm with Tiger-Riding Stance   fig. 679
跨虎挑掌
40. The Invitation of the White Ape (The Double Grappling Hand with Monkey Stance) 白猿請客（中式步雙封手）   fig. 680
41. The right Round House Punch with Hill-Climbing Stance   fig. 681
登山右圈捶
42. The right Filing Fist with Hill-Climbing Stance   fig. 682
登山右挫捶
43. The Chopping Fist with Circle Entering Stance   fig. 683
入環斬腰
44. The right Reverse Palm with Hill-Climbing Stance   fig. 684
登山右反掌
45. The right Toppling Hand with Filching Stance   Fig. 685A–685B
偷步右蹬撲
46. The Grapple-Down with Cross Stance   fig. 686
扭馬坐盆
47. The Belly-Caving Punch with Circle Entering Stance   Fig. 687
入環窩肚捶
48. The Positive and Negative Palm with Hill-Climbing Stance (The Double Dispeling Palms) 登山陰陽掌   fig. 688
49. The Seven Star Waist-Chopping Palm   fig. 689
七星引針斬腰
50. The Ward off Palm with Tiger-Riding Stance   fig. 690–690A
跨虎挑掌
51. The Slip-Rolling Palm with Hill-Climbing Stance (I)   fig. 691A
登山滾漏掌（一）
52. The Slip-Rolling Palm with Hill-Climbing Stance (II)   fig. 692A–692B
登山滾漏掌（二）
53. The right Knee-Striking with claw-Binding   fig. 693
捆爪右頂膝
54. The Double Bumping Fist with Hill-Climbing Stance   fig. 694
登山雙撞捶
55. The Halting Palm with Hill-Climbing Stance   fig. 695
登山封掌
56. The Seven-Star right Lower Proping Kick   fig. 696
七星右低軋捶
57. The right Back Chopping Fist with Leg-Extracting Kick   fig. 697
揪腿右崩捶
58. The right Chopping Fist with Horse-Riding Stance   fig. 698
馬式右劈捶

59. The right Back Chopping Fist with Hill-Climbing Stance fig. 699
　　登山右崩捶
60. The Door-Shuttering Kick fig. 700
　　閉門腿（撩陰腿）
61. The Ward off Palm with Tiger-Riding Stance fig. 701
　　跨虎挑掌
62. The left straight Forward Punch with Hill-Climbing Stance fig. 702
　　登山左統捶
63. The right Elbow-Striking with Filching Stance fig. 703A — 703B
　　偷步右叠肘
64. The right Back Chopping Fist with Filching Stance fig. 704
　　偷步右崩捶
65. The right Straight Punch with Toppling Stance fig. 705
　　偷彈右統捶
66. The left Round House Punch with Hill-Climbing Stance fig. 706
　　登山左圈捶
67. The right Power-Forcing Fist with Tiger-Riding Stance fig. 707
　　跨虎右勢捶
68. The Door-Shuttering Kick fig. 708
　　閉門腿（撩陰腿）
69. The Whip-Rolling Hand with Circle Entering Stnace fig. 709
　　入環滾捞手
70. The right Straight Forward Punch with Hill Climbing Stance fig. 710
　　登山右統捶
71. The Mantis catches the Cicada fig. 711
　　螳螂捕蟬
72. End with Attention Stance fig. 712 — 712B
　　中平收息

641 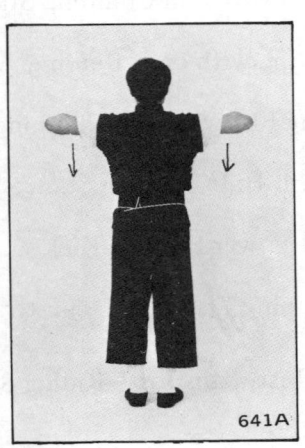　　　　　　641A 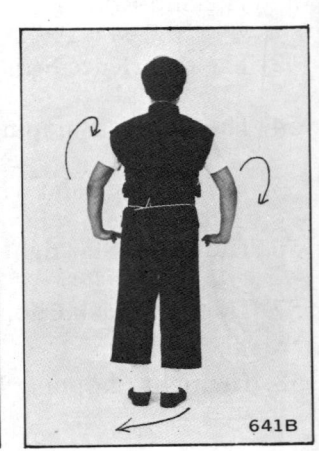　　　　　　641B

182

641C 641D 641E
642 643 644
644A 644B 645

646

647

648

649

650

651

651A

651B

652

184

653
654
655
656A
656
656
657
658
659

185

660 661 662

662A 663 663A

664 665 666

667

668

669

670A

670B

671

672

673

674

187

675A
675B
675C
676
677
678
679
680
681

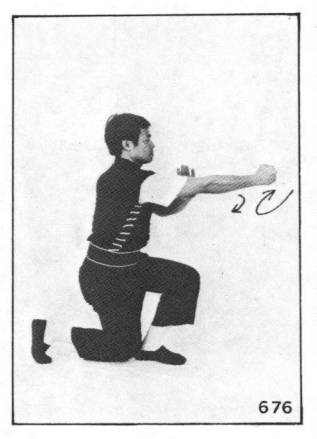

188

682 683 684
685A 685B 686
687 688 689

189

690 　690A 　691A

692A 　692B 　693

694 　695 　696

190

697 698 699
700 701 702
703A 703B 704

191

705

706

707

708

709

710

711

712A

712B

Explanation For Extracted Skills From The Mantis out of Its cave

THE MANTIS BOUBLE INTERCEPT HAND 螳螂雙臂勾
Figure 713–715 shows Master Lee raises his Double intercepted Hand to grasp down the opponent's coming attack with a Tiger—Riding Stance, at he same time he raises his left leg to kick at the opponent's waist part.

THE DOUBLE HAND—PUSHING WITH TOPPLING STANCE
蹬撲雙推手

Figure 716–720 shows Master Lee grasps the opponent's attacking hand with his left hand, while he pushes his right hand to halt at the opponent's left shoulder, at the same time, he raises his right leg to prop backward at the lower part of the opponent's front leg, so as to cause the opponent lose his balance.

716

717

718

719

194

THE LING PUNCH WITH HORSE—RIDING STANCE 馬式鑽捶
Figure 721—722 shows Master Lee pushes aside his left upturned palm at the opponent's elbow joint, at the same time, he twist his left fist to punch at the opponent's ribs.

THE DOUBLE BUMPING FIST WITH HILL-CLIMBING 登山雙撞捶

Figure 723–725 shows Master Lee turns both of his halting fist downward, while he launches a double straight punch at the opponent's front chest.

Method of Iron - Sand Palm Training

IRON-SAND PALM 鐵沙掌
The Seven-Star Mantis Style practising Series gives flexible variation of the motivated body, and the Respiratory Attainment of the Eighteen Arham enhances a strong human body. However, an adequate auxiliary with medical materials for training of the Iron-Sand Palm can make half way to success.

METHOD OF PHYSICAL STRENGTH TRAINING
A. **Sand Bag Method**（沙袋打法）(fig. R14 – R23)
   1. Face-down claping Method
   2. Back-down claping Method
   3. Palm-Chopping Mehtod

R14 R15 R16
R17 R18 R19
R20 R21 R22

B. **Sand-Inserting Method** (插沙法) (R24 – R35)
   1. Finger-Palm thrusting Method
   2. Fist-Hold Extracting Method
   3. Hand-Letting punch Method

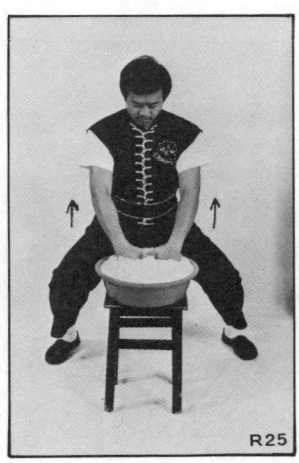

199

R27 R28 R29

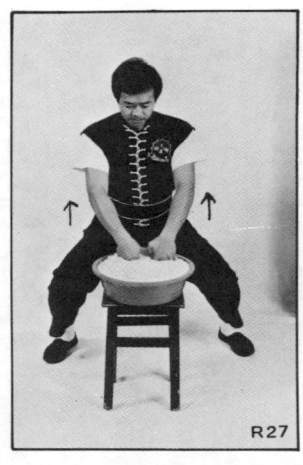

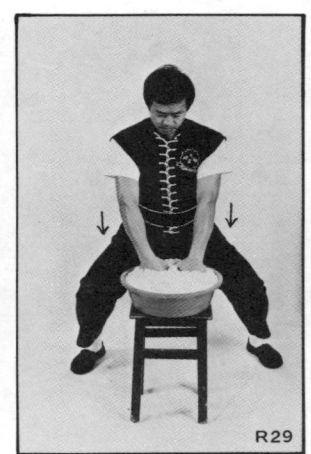

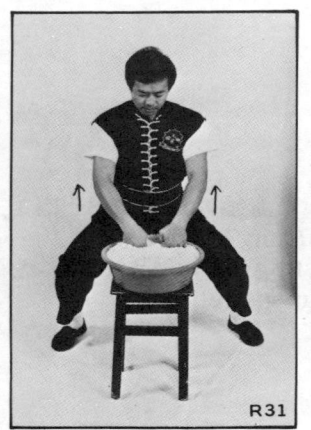

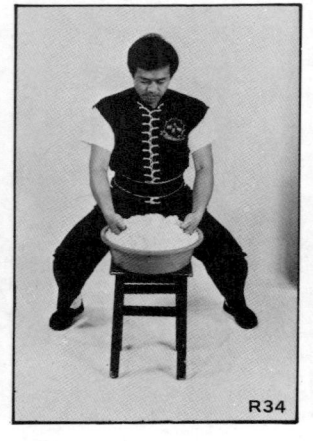

R30 R31 R32

R33 R34 R35

The Conventional Chinese Medical Prescription of Shaolin Monastery for Iron - Sand Palm Training

ZI WAN	(Aster tataricus L.)	柴苑	30g
LANG DU	(Autumn lycoctonum L.)	狼毒	30g
BAN XIA	(Pinellia tuberifera Ten)	半廈	30g
LONG GU	(Fossil of Dinosaur bone)	龍骨	30g
HUA JIAO	(Zanthoxylum bungeanum)	花椒	30g
TANG GU XIAO	(Thunbergia grandiflora Roxb.)	通骨消	30g
HAI SHI	(Pumic)	海石	30g
DI DING	(Chinensis G. Dom.)	地丁	30g
SHE CHUANG ZI	(Selinum japonicum Miq.)	蛇床子	30g
SHAN XIAO DING	(Corrusive iron-pin)	生銹鐵丁	100g
NAN SING	(Arisaema amurense Maxim)	南星	30g
HE TSU	(Black vinegar)	黑醋	5000g
SAN YIM	(Salt)	生鹽	30g
DI GU PI	(Lycinm Chinese Mill)	地骨皮	30g
CHUAN WU	(Aconitum carmichaeli)	川烏	30g
CHAO WU	(Aconitum Kusnezoffii)	草烏	30g
LAU WONG	(Brimstone)	硫磺	30g
BAI BU	(Stemona japonica)	百部	30g
LI LO	(Verairum nigrum L.)	藜蘆	30g

- For external only.
- When use, boiling up 15 minutes, become warm then put the hands inside until to cold after that don't washing, about one hour later can was.
- Every time when useing just boil up again.

The Application of Palm - fighting Technique

THE HALTING PALM 封掌
Figure 225–227 shows Master Lee draws his right forearm downward as he arrests the coming attack, at the same time he grapples the arrested coming attack with his left hand and release his right hand to pump ahead.

THE REVERSE PALM 反掌
Figure 228–229 shows Master Lee circles his right hand in front to strike downward with the back of his left palm while he grapples the coming attack with his left hand.

THE MILLSTONE PALM 磨盆掌

Figure 230–232 shows Master Lee draws his right hand backward while he holds the coming attack with his left hand, at the same time he forces his right palm toward the front.

THE SLIP–ROLLING PALM 滾漏掌

Figure 233–235 shows Master Lee circles his palms to press down the coming attack with his left palm, at the same time he points his stretched right palm toward the front.

THE SKIM OFF PALM 脫掌

Figure 236–238 shows Master Lee forces his left hand to discard the grappling hand from his opponent.

Demonstration for Weapons of The Seven - Star Mantis Style

Figure 1. Red Tasselslance
Figure 2. Kwan Knife
Figure 3. Three Joint Stick
Figure 4. Willow Leaves Single Knife
Figure 5. Big Knife
Figure 6. Nine Joint Steel Whip
Figure 7. Willow Leaves Double Knife
Figure 8. Tiger Head Double Hook
Figure 9. Fong Tin Lance
Figure 10. Double Seven-Star Cane
Figure 11. Double Seven-Star Hammer
Figure 12. Seven-Star Single Sword
Figure 13. Long Stick
Figure 14. Tiger Hook
Figure 15. Seven-Star Drum

206

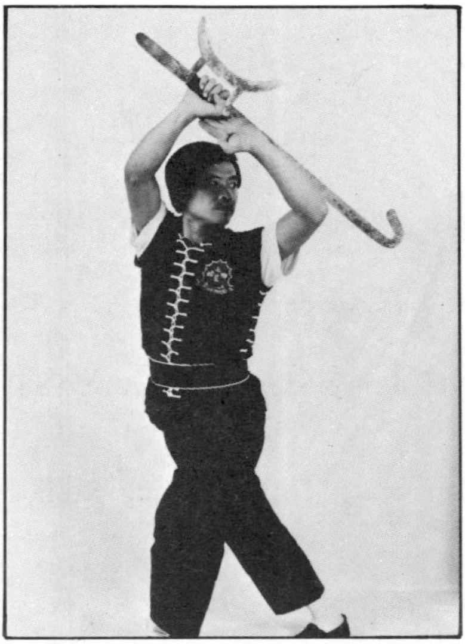

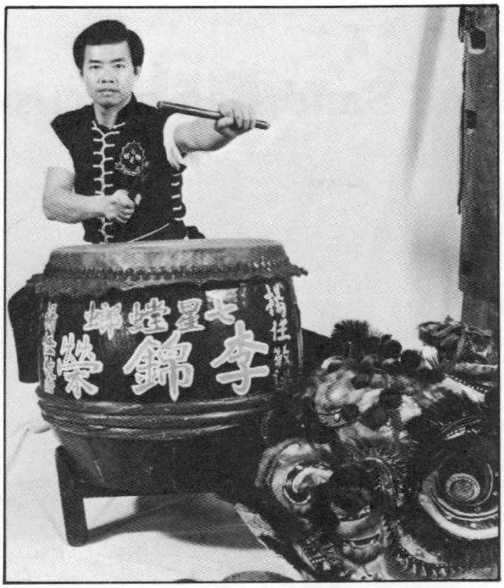
七星螳螂
李錦榮

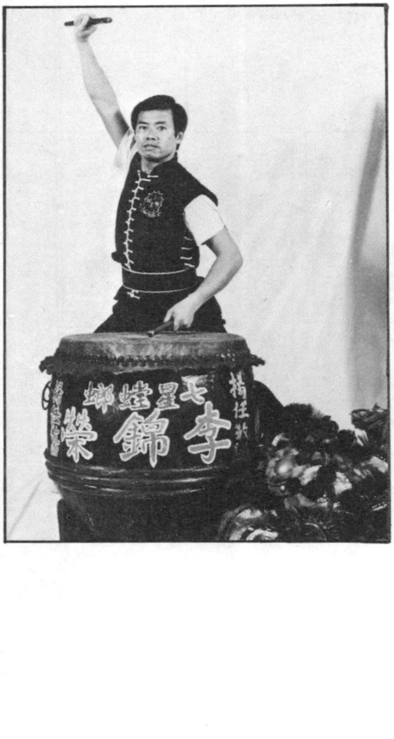
七星螳螂
李錦榮

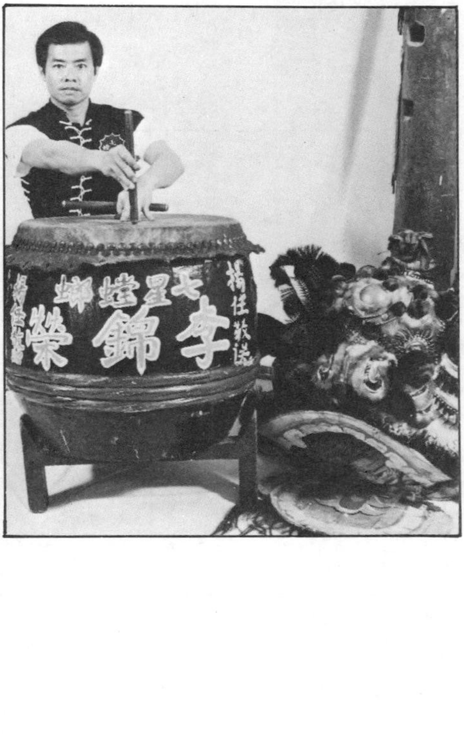
七星螳螂
李錦榮
楊任敬送

The Sand Bag practising

1. Straight Forward punch left and right. (figure 586-587)

2. Knee-Striking left and right with Leg-Hanging Stance. (figure 588-589)

3. Horizontal Elbow-Striking left and right with Hill-Climbing Stance (figure 590-591)

4. Horizontal Leg-Sweeping left and right. (figure 592-593)

5. Door-Shuttering Kick left and right. (figure 594-595)

589

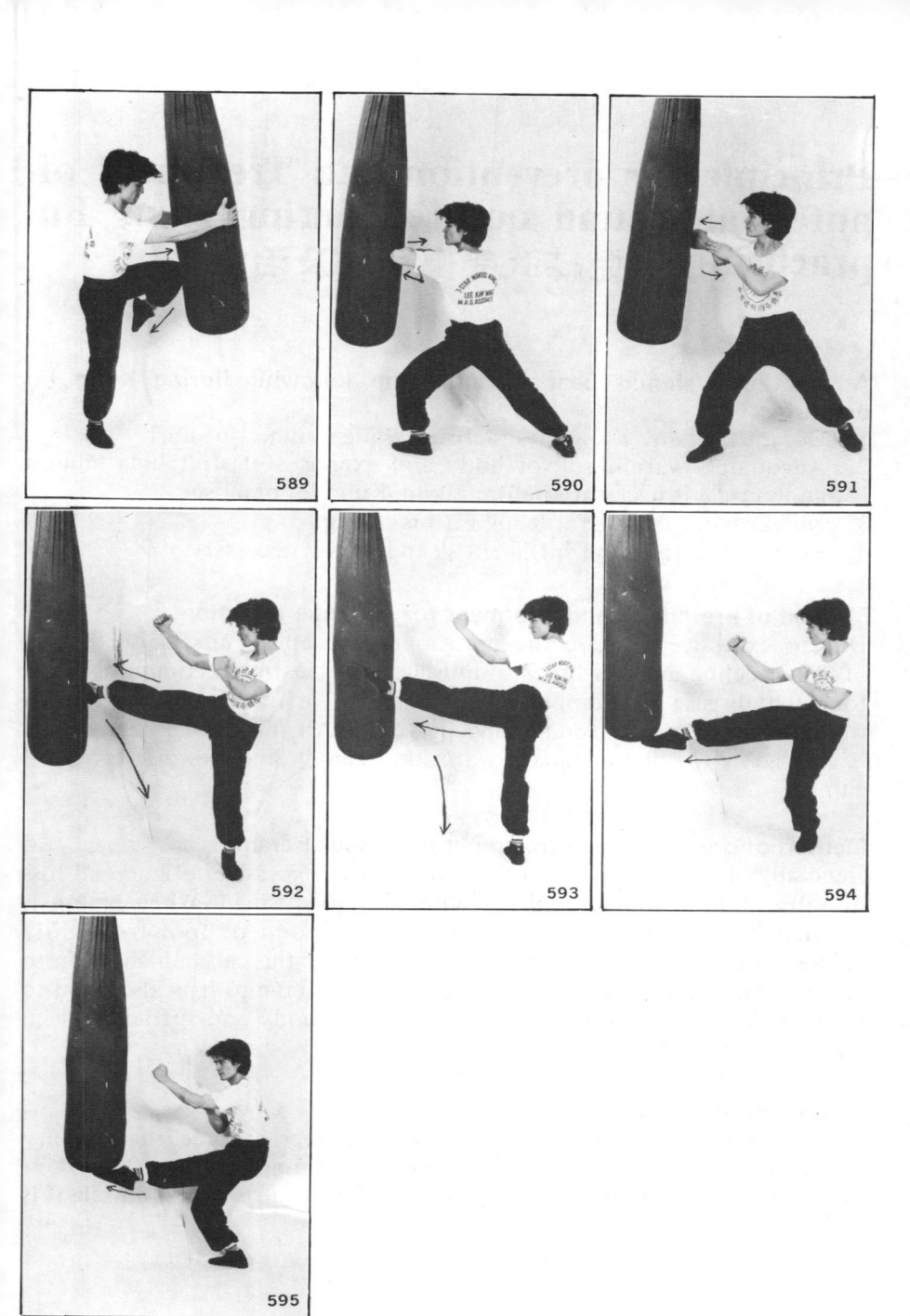

590

591

592

593

594

595

Principle for prevention and Treatment of potential wound occured during Kung Fu practising 避免練武受傷預防及治療

A practioner should bear in mind the following during Kung Fu practising.
1. Do not take any Kung Fu Practising while in illness or hurt.
2. Adequately warming up of body and exercise for stretching tendon and muscle is necessary before taking Kung Fu practise.
3. No excessive fatique for Kung Fu practising.
4. Regular live time and sufficient sleep hours is necessary.

Method of prevention and treatment for muscular infection
Due to excessive exercise the pratitioner will apear muscular infection of red sweeling and hard pain of muscle. The treatment commonly used for such disease is to apply regular massage of muscle and bath with warm water are good for making prevention of muscular infection. It is also good to take adequate warm up of body and exercise for stretching.

Mehtod of prevention and treatment of muscular cramp
Generally muscular cramp will be occured in excessive fatigue and loss of salts in human body during Kung Fu practising. When cramp is occured in the calf, it is help to up lift the point of foot by slightly facing it upward, so as to stretch the muscle of the calf. In addition to give regular massage for treatment fo muscular cramp, it is also good to take adequate exercise for warming up of the body and sufficient sleep hours.

Treatment of muscular traumatism
As wound is occured by getting bump from external force, the capillary vessels are being cracked and the museles are being teared off in excessive tensioning. At the early begining of getting hurts of the muscle it is

hely to use ice-cooling treatment for preventing continuously loss of inner blood from vessels of the interior body. The subsequent effectively method is to treat externally with chinese osteopathy medical wine.

Treatment of dislocation of shoulder joint
The assistant first to hold firmly at opposit side of the patient's injured part, then he pulls the patient's body toward an opposit direction against the physician, at the same time, the physician pulls toward another direction while keeping the patient's body steadily and sloppingly toward the inflected part.

As the physician gives his assistant a signal for pulling at the opposit direction, he turns the patient's arm backward at the shoulder joint for treating a front dislocation of the shoulder joint or he turns the Patient's arm forward at the shoulder joint for treating a rear dislocation of the shoulder joint. After the humerus head is being pulled out, the physician raise his kneecap to bracket upward at the humerus head untill a 'knock' sound is being heard, then at this time, the humerus head is slipped into the joint, and dislocation of shoulder joint is restored.

It is noted that if the dislocation of the shoulder joint is dislocated backward the patient's upper arm should be stretched outward at 60 to 80 degree with the shoulder head and lifted upward at a 30 degree for processing a counter-pulling action, at the end of such action, the physician turns the patien's arm forward while he props his thumb at humerus head toward the front, then restoration for dislcoated shoulder joint is completed.

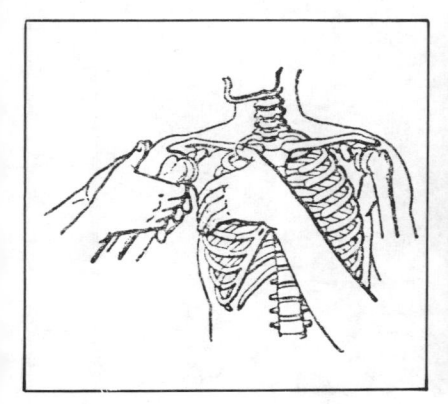

Treatment of dislocation of elbow joint

The patient sits to let the assistant use both of his hands to hold at middle part of the patient's arm, the physician stands aside by the patient with one hand holds at the patient's wrist and another hand places on the humerus at elbow joint, at the same time, the physician and his assistant pull either side respectively, while the physician bends the patient's elbow joint with his hand on the patient's wrist, in order to push down the patient's humerus as the elbow joint is bent at a certain degree, a slipping 'knock' sound is heard and restoration for the dislocated elbow joint is completed.

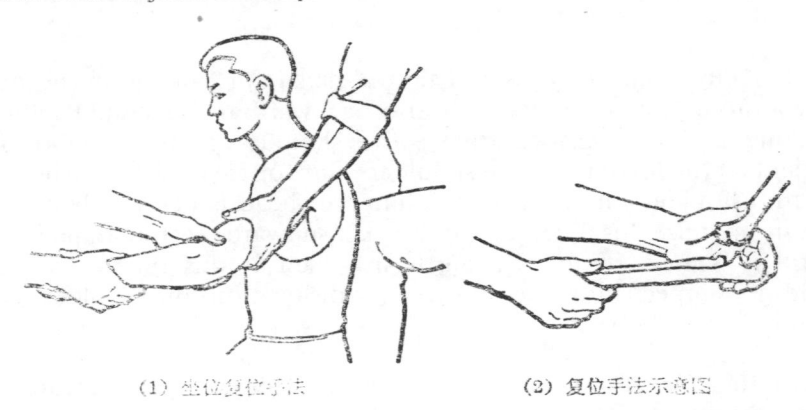

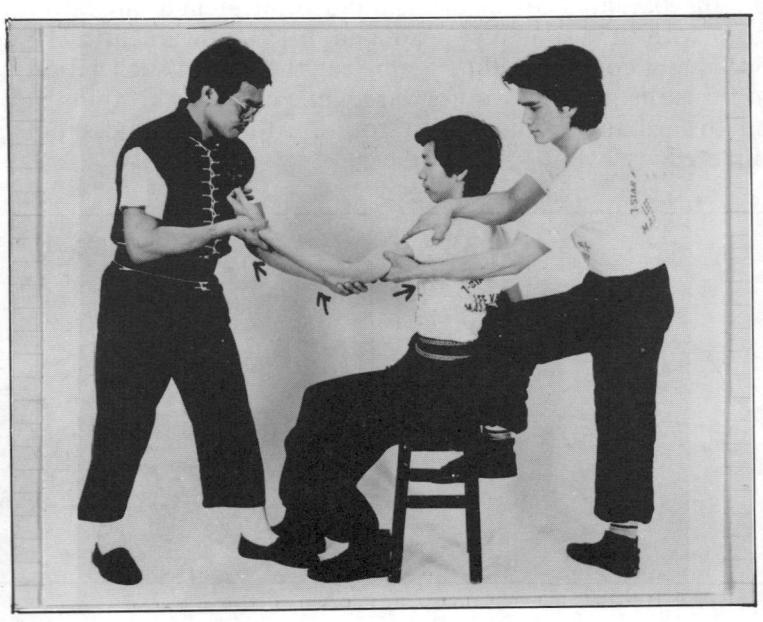

(1) 坐位复位手法　　　　(2) 复位手法示意图

Analysis and Application of the Vital point striking and position of caves in Acupuncture
點脈及針灸穴位療病之分析

Parts of the position of caves in acupuncture can give effective on treating disease under adequate treatment, however, wounds will be occured when giving excessive attack on position of caves.

Methods of vital point attacking at position of caves in acupuncture.
1. Cave – striking
2. Cave – capturing
3. Cave – puncturing
4. Cave – pressing

It is noted that the position of Cheung Mon is the most dangerous one among the position of caves which is located in the spleem. It is danger to life, when the spleem is being attack which can cause an opponent yet loss of inner-blood seriously.

EXTRACTED EXAMPLES FOR POSITION OF CAVES 部份穴位實例
THE CHIHTSE 只澤穴位
The position of CHIHTSE is located at the elbow crease on the lateral border of the tendon of the bicep brachii muscle.

Main Effort in Disease Treatment
Cough, pain occured in throat and muscle of the arm near elbow joint, and fever.
Acupuncture needle – puncturing one inch up to five minutes.
When the CHIHTSE is being pressed it will occure a paralysed pain. Power-Chopping punch in the Seven-Star Mantis Style is an example of Cave-striking at the CHIHTSE, this can cause an opponent feels paralysed pain at position of the CHIHTSE and weaken the opponent's attacking effort.

CHIHTSE

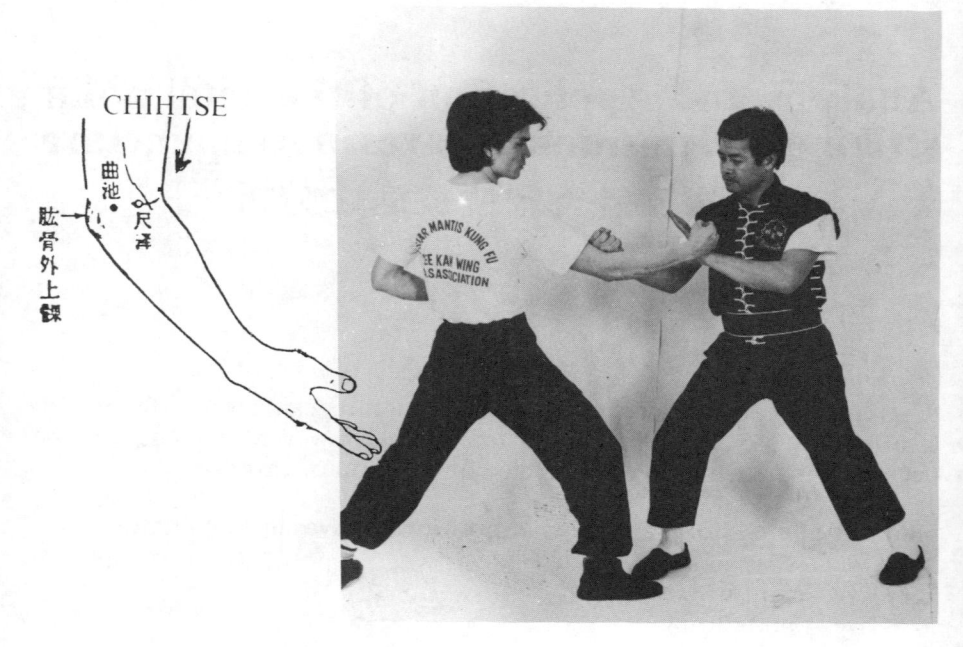

曲池
尺
肱骨外上髁

fig. 1

THE CHUCHIH 曲池穴
The position of CHUCHIH is located at the external end of the elbow crease as the elbow is flexed.

Main Effort in Disease Treatment
Pain occured in elbow joint, high fever, hypertension, high blood pressure, partial paralysis, itchy skin.
Acupuncture needle-puncturing 1½ inches up to 8 minutes.
The invitation of the White Apes in the Seven-Star Mantis Style is an example of caves-capturing at the CHUCHIH. This can cause the opponent feels paralysed pain at the position of the CHUCHIH.

CHUCHIH

fig. 2

THE YIFENG 翳風
The position of YIFENG is located behind the lobule of the auricle, in the depression between the mastoid process and the mandible.

Main Effort in Disease Treatment
Deaf, Buzzing in the ears, paralysis of neurosis of face.
Acupuncture needle-puncturing at corner of mouth one inch up to 5 minutes.
The Millstone Palm in the Seven-Star Mantis Style is an example of Cave-puncturing or caves-pressing at the YIFENG. Since the position of YIFENG having by pass of vein and Artery, when the YIFENG is being attacked this can cause the opponent feels faint or even being died.

YIFENG

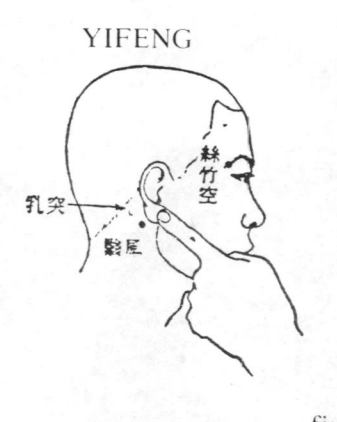

fig. 3

fig. 3A

THE TAI YAN 太陽穴
The TAI YAN is located at the outer edge of the eye-bow, which has distribution of vein.

Main Effort in Disease Treatment
Headache and catch cold.
The "Upper Round-House Punch" in the Seven-Star Mantis Style is an example of Cave-pressing at TAI YAN.
The importance of above examples of caves in acupuncture as explained in the anatomy is because of the Exsistence of vein and Artery and the nervous system nearby. When an opponent is being wounded by concentrated force, effort of disease treatment can be achieved with adequate and corrected application.

THE TAI YAN

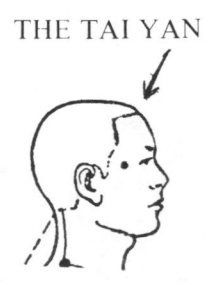

fig. 4 A

fig. 4 B

218

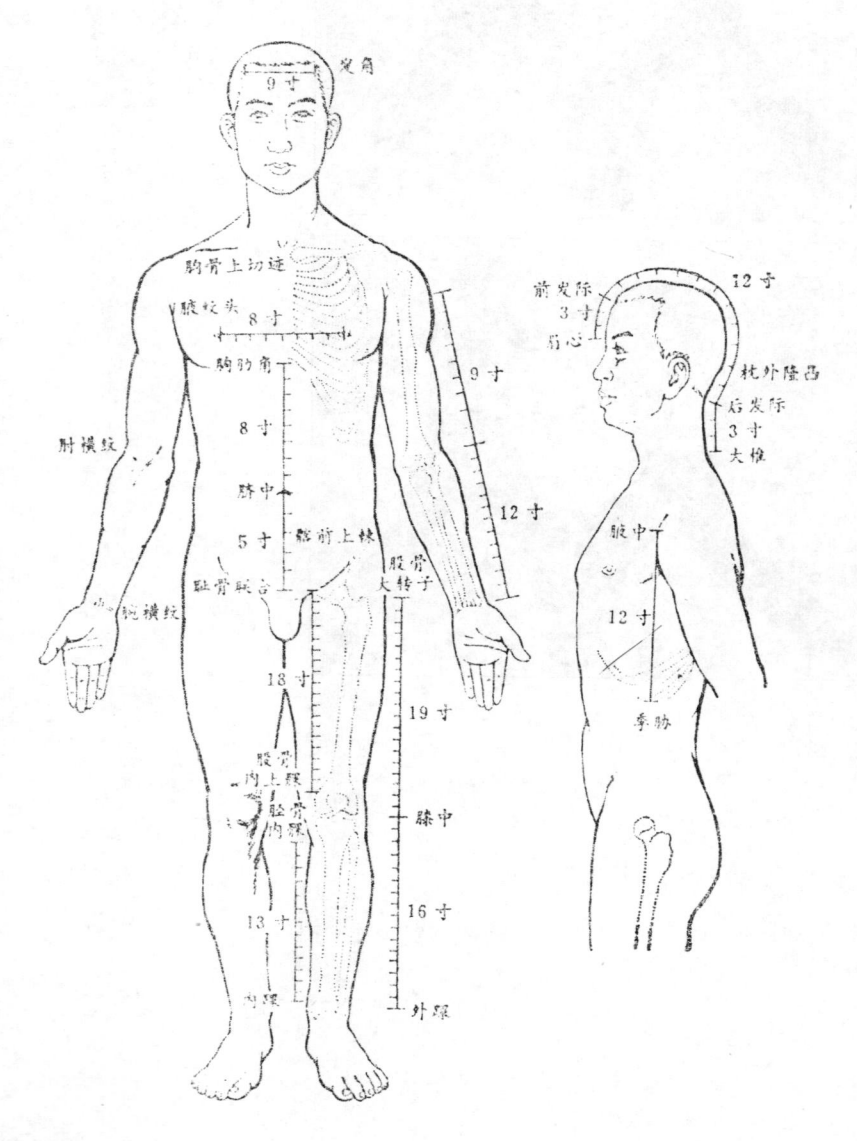

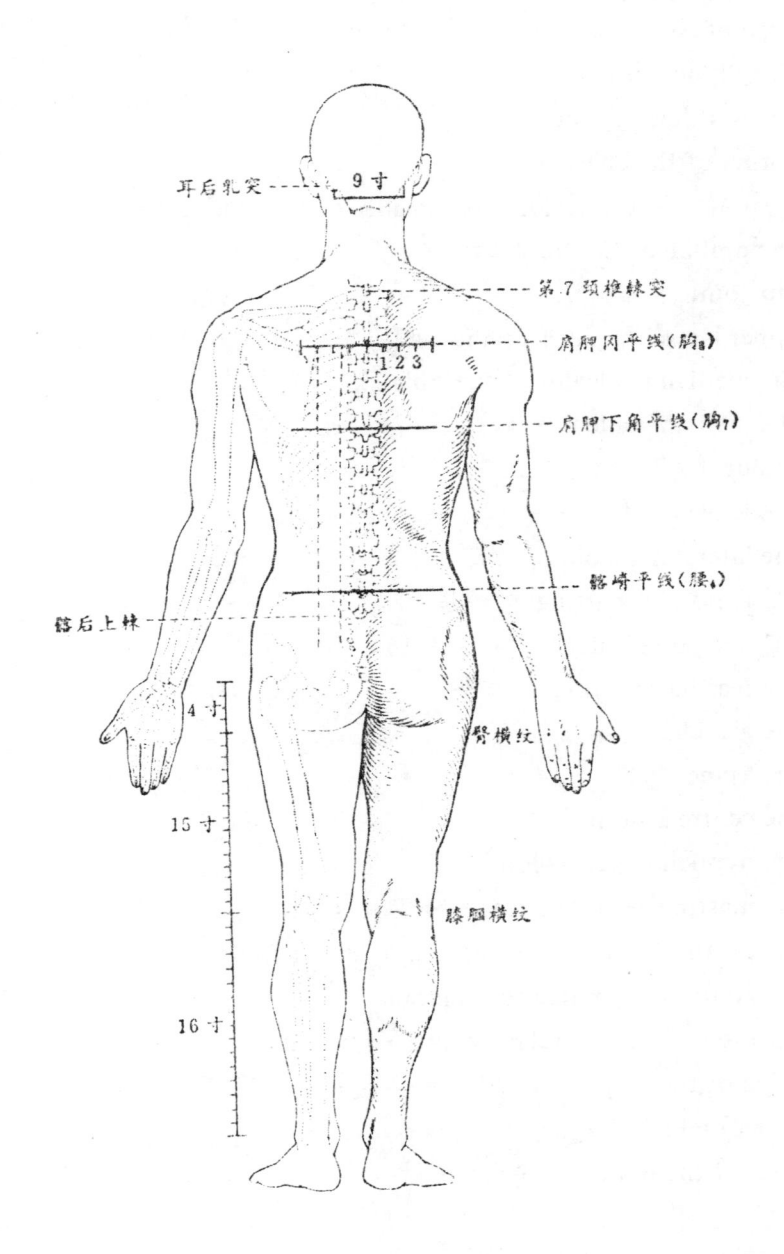

1. The corner of the forehead 髮角
2. The upper Horizontal line
   of the sternal 胸骨上切迹
3. Head of the axillary line 腋紋頭
4. The elbow line 肘橫紋
5. The wist line 腕橫紋
6. Corner of the chest rib 胸肋角
7. In front of the anterior superior iliac spine 髂前上棘
8. The umbilicus Centre 臍中
9. Hip joint 耻骨聯合
10. Upper lateral mallealus femur 股骨內上踝
11. The median mallealus of the tibia 股骨內髁
12. The median mallealus 內踝
13. Femur 股骨大轉子
14. The Knee Centre 膝中
15. The lateral malleolus 外踝
16. The front hair parting 前髮際
17. The occiput eminence 枕外隆凸
18. The rear hair parting 後髮際
19. The glabella 眉心
20. The Spine 大椎
21. The centre armpit 腋中
22. The hypochodriac region 季肋
23. The mastoid region of rear ears 耳後乳突
24. Process the 7th Cervical Vetebra 第7頸椎棘突
25. Horizontal line joining the spinous
    processes of the scapular 肩胛岡平綫（胸$_3$）
26. Angle of the scapular 肩胛下角平綫（胸$_7$）
27. Horizontal line joining the upper
    edges of the ilium 髂嵴平綫（腰$_4$）
28. Behind the exterior
    iliac spine 髂後上棘
29. Gluteal flow 臀橫紋
30. The horizontal line
    of the rear of Knee
    joint 膝膕橫紋

The Respiratory Attainment of the Eighteen Arhan 十八羅漢氣功

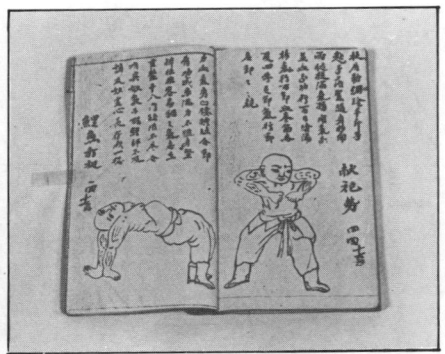

The Respiratory Attainment of the Eighteen Arhan including Five parts of the standard style of the Shaolin Monastery. The purpose is designed for training a strong human body, and giving a good practising method for training good function of the human body which is to create a prosperous body and to reduce illness into minimum.

The following extracted 3 parts with 14 styles and 120 movements are introduced as a Basic Practising Method.

It is preferably to select a place with good natural ventilation for practising excercise but doing an excercise against a fan is not recommended.

Excercise can be made in the morning or evening, which is suitable for young and elder people, whenever in practising, breath is slow but not heavy, and breath is continous without stopping. After a complete practising, the practitioner can feel a hot air which is diffused out from the human body, and massive sweat is being appeared. This is also particularly a good exercise for restoring bronchitis.

It is noted that cold water is not suitable for drink, but a boiled warm water is recommended.

Mehtod of practising for THE RESPIRATORY ATTAINMENT OF THE EIGHTEEN ARHAN PART I. (The Fairy Folds Hand) 仙人拱手

Style I
Hands pushing forward with attention stance. 雙手直推雙腳並立
1. to hold fist by waist side.
2. Keeping eyes sight ahead.
3. to breath naturally and lick the point of the tongue at the teeth ridge.

   (fig. J1– J12)

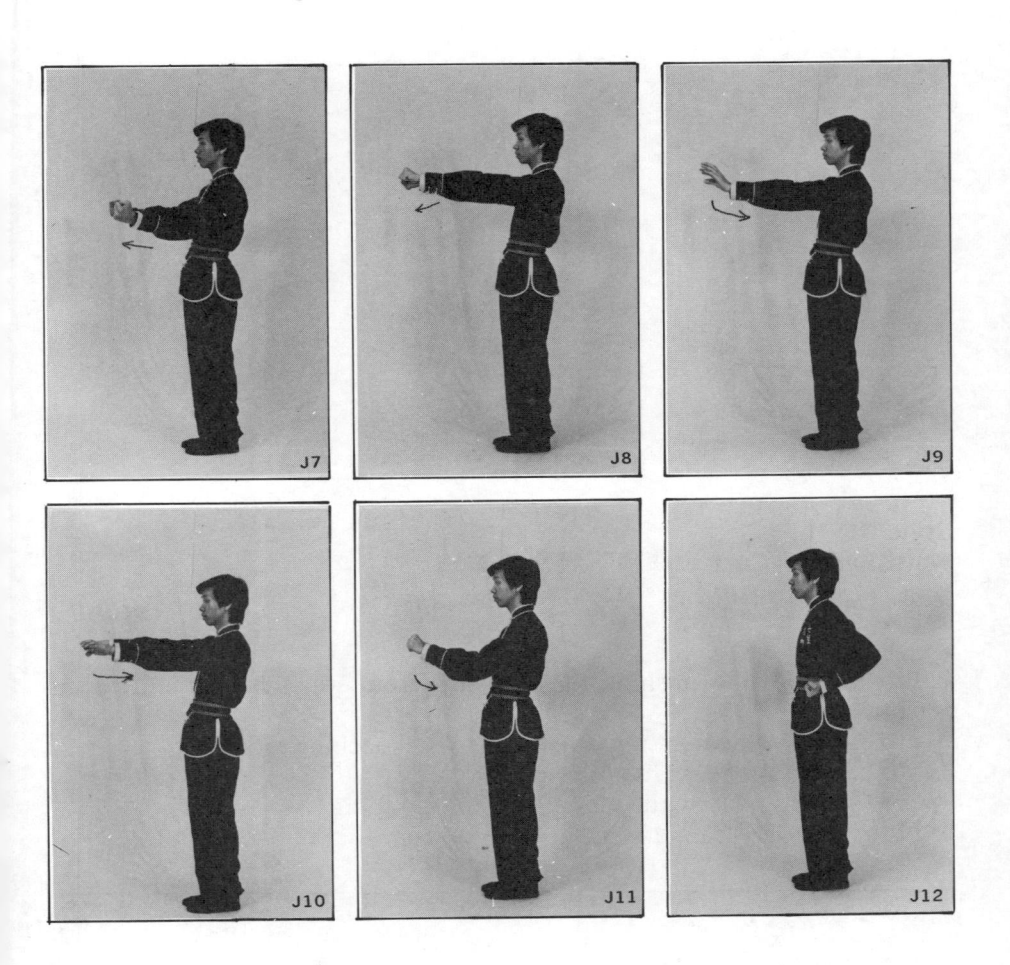

Style II
Hands overturning and pushing up at one breath. 翻手舉鼎一口氣
(Fig. J13 – J14)

1. to exhale while pushing up fists from waist-side to the shoulder height.
2. to grasp the stretched fingers to form a fist and inhale again.
3. to inhale while drawing fists slowly back to the waist side.
4. to repeat the same of the movement from 1–3 for 20 times.

Style III
Waist-Bending Curtsy 曲膝下腰伏俯施禮
(Fig. J15—J18)

1. to inhale while pushing fists upward from waist height and facing upward.
2. to exhale while bending waist to let fists reaching ground.
3. to circle fists outward above ground.
4. to breath slowly while picking up the catching fist.
5. to repeat the same from 1—4 for 20 times.

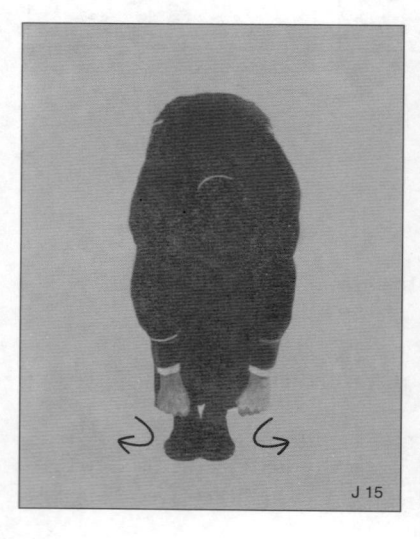

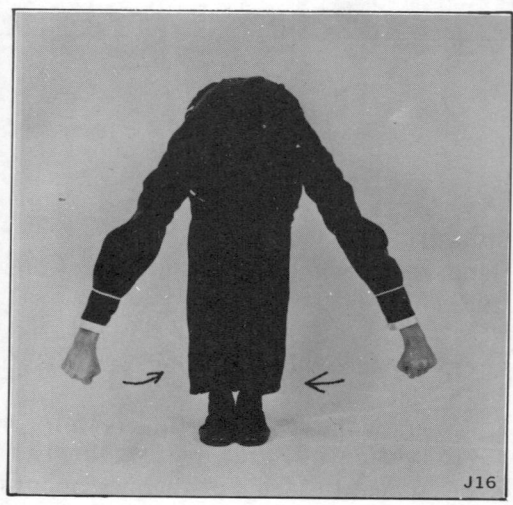

Style IV
Upward face Moving Sun with Concaved waist and Convexed belly.
(Fig. J19-J28) 仰面朝天凹腰腆肚

1. to change fists into upturned palm while reaching fists at above head.
2. to keeps the same with breath naturally and face upward for a certain period.
3. to feel a flow of warm air from the forearm to the point of fingers.
4. to exhale while lowering plams.

J19C J20 J21
J22 J23
J24 J25

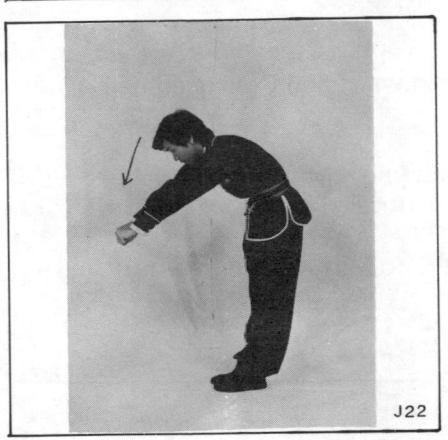

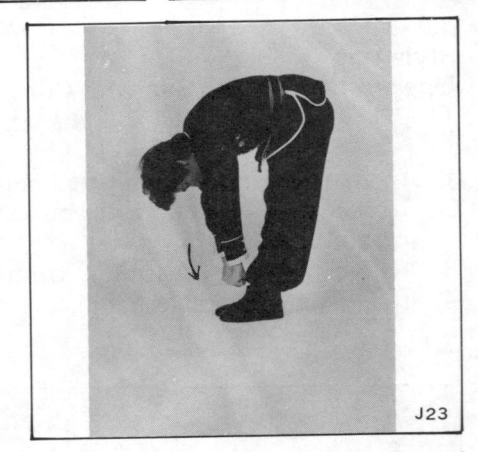

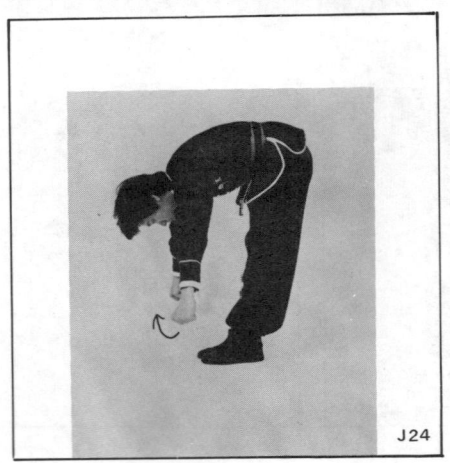

J26

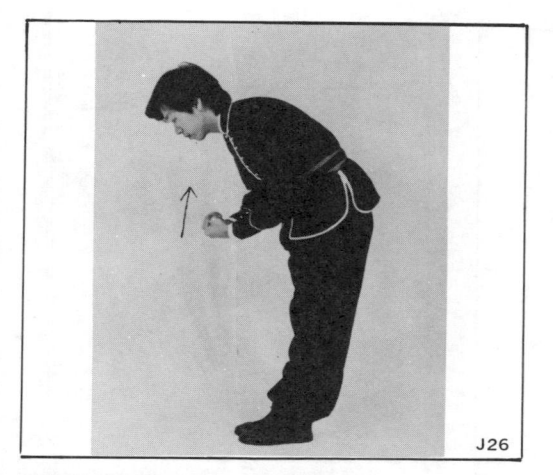

J27

J28

PART II
THE SUPREME CHIEF RAISES-TRIPOD 霸王舉鼎

STYLE I — Matching hands with Striving Stance. 雙手分水，兩腿掙力 (K4—K8)

1. to spread apart legs in align with a straight line while the point of foots facing left and right.
2. to join the palm together in front of the chest.
3. to lick the point of the tongue at the teeth ridge and keeping the eyes sight ahead while taking breath naturally.

227

K4

K5

K6

K7

K8

228

雙搥分磋，搬鞍騎馬
STYLE 2 — Hands impeding and Horse Riding (K9— K11)
1. to inhale while stretching the upturned palms slowly toward left and right respectively.
2. to exhale while circling the upturned hands and joining the palms again.
3. to repeat the same for 20 times.

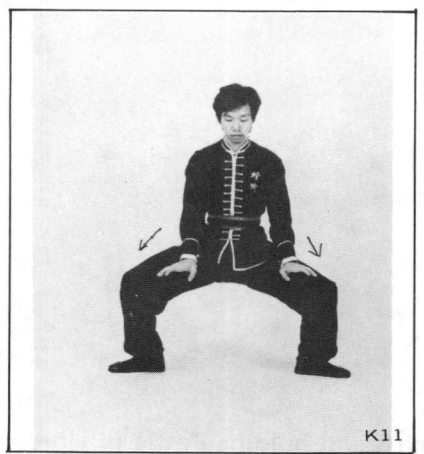

K9

K10

K11

大鵬挺翅，全身使力
STYLE 3 — The Roc Stretches Wings. (K12— K14)
1. to inhale while holding fists to punch straightly downward and keeping a vertical body.

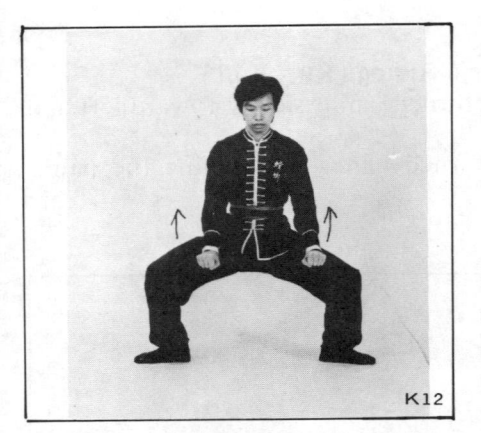

力舉千斤，提杵騎馬
STYLE 4 — Forcing up thousand weights and holding Pestle in Horse-Riding (K15—K16)
1. To grasp hands outward.
2. to inhale while raising fists upward at same level of shoulders and elbows.
3. to punch fists downward.
4. to repeat the same for 20 times.

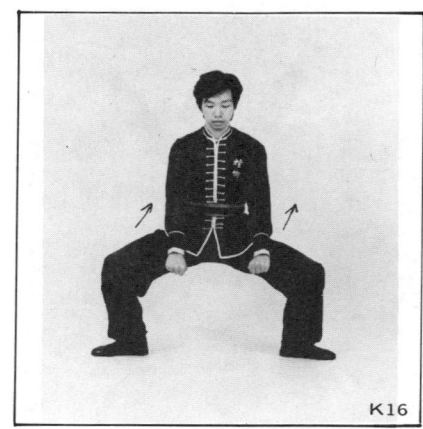

STYLE 5 — The Golden Plate holds the moon with total Force. (K17, K18, K19, K20, K21 K22, K23.) 金盤托月，全身精力

1. to change fists into palms while bracketing palms upward and pointing fingers at left and right respectively.
2. to breath naturally and staying for a certain period.
3. to turn palm inward while laying the horizontal palms downward and holding an attention stance.
4. completion of part II.

231

K19

K20

K21

K22

K23

PART III
FLOWER-INSERTING LEFT AND RIGHT 左右插花
雙手扶鉅，兩腳並立
STYLE I — Great-Proping Hands (K24, K25, K26, K27, K28, K29.)
1. holding fists at waist sides with Attention Stance and look at the right.
2. to exhale while pushing out upturned palms front and back to the right with right Hill-Climbing Stance and turning head from the right to the left.
3. to exhale while grasping hand into fists at the waist sides and turning head right and left.
4. to repeat same movement for 20 times.

仙人指路騎馬
STYLE 2 — The Fairy Shows Way. (K30, K31, K32, K33, K34, K35)
1. to repeat the same from action 1 to 3 of style 1 by the reverse direction.
2. to practise the same for 20 times.

234

單手過腦，偏氣實腹
STYLE 3 — Single Hand hunting up and down(L1, L2, L3, L4, L5, L6, L7.)

1. to place fists at the waist side with Horse-Riding Stance.
2. to raise up the left hand while pressing down the right hand and breath naturally.
3. to chop down left fist while raising up the right fist and breath naturally.
4. to repeat the same for 20 times.

L3

L4

L5

L6

L7

垂鈎抱腿，曲膝勾腳
STYLE 4 — Downward Hook with Seven-Star Stance (L8,—L18.)
1. to bend the horizontal left arm upward, while hooking down the right arm at the waist side with a right Hill-Climbing Stance.
2. to exhale while bending the waist to reach the left arm at the point of the foot.
3. to draw up the body and repeat the same for 20 times.
4. to practise the same movement at the reverse direction.

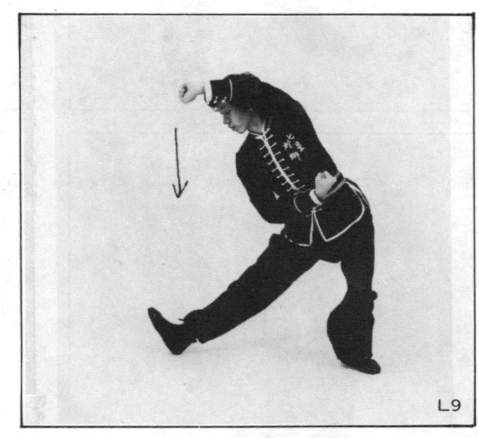

238

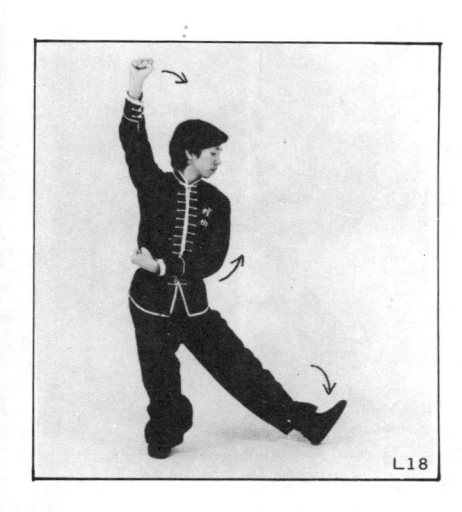

雙手交合，收功提氣
STYLE 5 — Hand-Matching and take breath easily. (L19—L26)
1. to bend the right horizontal arm upward with a Hill-Climbing Stance.
2. to bracket both palms upward while placing the left palm at the head's level and placing the right palm at shoulder's level.
3. holding the above action for a certain period until both legs are feeling tired.
4. to repeat the same movement by the right hand side and breath naturally for a certain period until both legs are feeling tired.
5. to exhale while taking an Attention Stance.
6. to bend the horizontal elbows at the shoulder's height and laying the horizontal palm downward.

L21

L22

L23

L24

L25

L26

240